D1123641

*The*
# TENORS

# The
# TENORS

EDITED BY

*Herbert H. Breslin*

MACMILLAN PUBLISHING CO., INC.
*New York*

Grateful acknowledgment is made to Alfred A. Knopf, Inc., for permission to quote the excerpts on pages 46 and 47, from *Responses* by David Cairns, © 1973.

Macmillan Publishing Co., Inc.
866 Third Avenue, New York, N. Y. 10022
Collier-Macmillan Canada Ltd.

Library of Congress Cataloging in Publication Data

Breslin, Herbert H    comp.
    The tenors.

    CONTENTS: Bender, W. Richard Tucker.—Ardoin, J. Jon Vickers.—Downs, J. Franco Corelli.—Rich, A. Placido Domingo.—Rubin, S. E. Luciano Pavarotti.
    1. Singers—Biography. I. Title.
ML400.B745T4    782.1'092'2 [B]    74-11332
ISBN 0-02-515000-6

FIRST PRINTING 1974

Printed in the United States of America

# Contents

*The*
# TENORS

# Preface

As a professional public relations manager, I have spent a lot of years alerting the national press to the doings of singers, pianists, conductors, and others regarded as celebrities in the field of "serious" music. It is hard to break the habit of publicizing artists, even when the artists in question are not officially one's own clients.

There are many reasons that I decided to ask five writers on musical subjects to dissect the art and personalities of five of today's great tenors. The first and most important reason is simply that they are all great singers and I admire them extravagantly. Their names, of course, are Franco Corelli, Placido Domingo, Luciano Pavarotti, Richard Tucker, and Jon Vickers. They are not the only five tenors in the world and they are not even the only great ones. None of them is perfect, though I think one or two come close. All are, in varying ways, great singers and great personalities, and each is capable of arousing great feelings in his audiences. I have a feeling that apologies are due some other tenors who did not find a place in this collection. Apologies are hereby offered, with the perfectly honest excuse that no container is big enough to contain everything. I thought it better to be exhaustive rather than all-inclusive, to do justice to a few rather than injustice to many.

Another reason for this book is that all these tenors are, indisputably, male. There has never been, to the best of my knowledge, a collection of personality profiles on male singers. Prima donnas, yes—but the great female singers have been so extolled and idolized to the exclusion of men that there are not even male equivalents of the words *diva* or *prima donna.* (Well, in purely grammatical terms, there are, but who ever uses them?) I hope I will not be accused of male chauvinism—a phrase much in use at the time of this writing—when I say that it is far easier to get any woman's name into print than it is to get a man's.

Most editors are men, and most of them have a healthy appreciation of female attributes. If a prima donna is blessed with good looks and the ability to recite quips into reporters' microphones, publicity is assured. On more than one occasion I have been asked to provide an entertaining story, simply to give an editor the excuse to run a picture of a pretty singer. I do not remember ever being told that an editor has found the photo of any male performer so irresistible that he absolutely must have an anecdote to go with the picture.

But the reasons for the preponderance of female performers in the news seem to me to go beyond the simple fact that male editors like pictures of females. It is certainly easier for a woman to dazzle her audiences (whether they are sitting in theaters or in newspaper offices) than it is for men. For one thing, women have the advantage of colorful dress. The bare shoulder, flash of bosom, swirl of gown, the wondrous hairdo that cleverly transforms the ordinary into the memorable—all these are priceless aids to whatever natural charisma the prima donna possesses. Male performers, deprived of such easy routes to fame, have to rely upon their talents, hiding their personalities behind the stern façades of tuxedos, tie and tails, or, at the very least, a coat and tie.

It is a historical fact that women have until very recently been held to a subservient position in society (and in many cultures still are), which gives them a position in most dramas that is capable of winning easy sympathy from an audience. The usual operatic heroine is a helpless creature, often victimized by men or betrayed by her emotional attachment to them. Tosca, for instance, begins to encounter problems the moment she falls in love with a man; her doom is sealed when she arouses the lust of another. Carmen, for all her liberatedness, is murdered by a man. Even Turandot, a domineering lady if there ever was one, finally submits meekly to Prince Calaf, presumably renouncing her leadership in a female-dominated government to live modestly as Calaf's wife.

Operas that revolve around a male are rare, and that male is usually an unpleasant one. Verdi was fond of the baritone voice, but his Simon Boccanegra, Rigoletto, and Falstaff, if not entirely unsympathetic, are certainly unattractive. Otello is an exception, but no matter how pitiful he becomes, it is Desdemona who wins the lasting sympathy of an audience. Whether Peter Grimes is destroyed by society or by his own brutality is an arguable point, but at least half of any audience always feels he deserves what he gets.

From the musical standpoint, nature itself has given the female sex an inestimable advantage: the female voice is placed an octave higher than the man's (at least in the field of "legitimate" singing). The smallest female voice, if properly produced, is nearly always audible and, in the proper roles, the smallness becomes a positive advantage. Witness the success of such famous sopranos as Amelita Galli-Curci, Lily Pons, Bidú Sayão, petite women all, with small voices that enhanced the impression of youth and innocence. The octave advantage gives women the ability to dominate massive choral and orchestral forces in a way impossible for any male. In the world of opera, nothing succeeds like high notes, and women have the highest ones.

At one time, things were different. Indeed, the first male singers to win the adulation of large publics were sopranos, occasionally altos. These were the castrati, a fortunately extinct line of male singers who had been castrated before puberty, the resulting physical development having the effect of preserving the boyish treble quality of their voices, while adding the full resource of a mature male physique. The reasons for the existence of the castrati were, ironically, due to the low estate held by women during that period (roughly, 1562–1850). Obeying such biblical injunctions as St. Paul's "Let your women keep silence in the churches" (1 Cor. 14:34) and St. Timothy's "Let the women learn in silence with all subjection . . . but I suffer not a woman to teach, nor to usurp authority over the man, but to be in silence" (1 Tim. 2:11–12), female singers were banned by the Church of Rome from singing in either churches or theaters.

In 1599, two Italian castrati were admitted to the Sistine Chapel and the age of great castrati was born. These geldings must have produced extraordinary sounds, far removed from anything uttered by today's countertenors. Imagine a boy's voice, grown to maturity with no loss of tone or lowering of pitch, supported by phenomenal lung capacity, and projected with the force of a masculine physique. The castrati could sustain a tone for more than one minute, could compete with trumpets, sail through coloratura passages of dizzying length and complexity, and display technical accomplishments that have been completely lost: the "hammerstroke," for instance, rapid, full-voiced repeated notes, which must have sounded rather like a vocalizing steam hammer. Trills and enormous leaps from high to low and back again, all executed at top speed, were other standard items in the castrati's technical armory.

Public taste for castrato singing, however, was finally exhausted and by the twentieth century general repugnance for the entire subject had set in. Audiences no longer would tolerate the sight of a grotesque-looking male (the operation, combined with strict vocal training, had drastic results on the physique) warbling in the soprano range and had, instead, developed a taste for the sound of the normal tenor voice.

Even this "normal" tenor voice differed from today's tenor, though. People wanted sweetness, not loudness, from their tenors. There were some very high notes demanded of tenors (right up to the F above high C!), but nobody expected a full-voiced top tone with full chest force under it. At around F below the high C, falsetto (or what we today would call falsetto) took over, and nobody expected anything different. Thus it was a sensation when, around 1820, Domenico Donzelli achieved the unheard-of feat of singing a mere high A in chest voice. Gilbert-Louis Duprez carried it up to top C in 1831 during a performance of Rossini's *William Tell*, startling Rossini, who likened the sound to "the squawk of a capon whose throat is being cut." When the next contender —Enrico Tamberlik, who had managed to reach a C-sharp— visited Rossini, the disapproving old composer told him to leave his C-sharp in the hallway and pick it up on his way out.

Today nobody disapproves of full-voiced tenoring. Indeed, the more stentorian qualities of the five gentlemen who are the subjects of this book have made them instantly appealing to so many people. I am as impressed by big, firm voices as anybody else, but it is not volume that makes me admire these men so strongly. What counts with Luciano Pavarotti are his energy, elegance, and brilliance. With Richard Tucker, it is his superb voice and a technical know-how that enables him to sing excitingly at an age when most of his contemporaries have bidden farewell to both voices and careers; Mr. Tucker thrilled me in 1945 and today, in 1974, he is still thrilling me. Franco Corelli is famous for his good looks (extremely rare in the tenor race, for some reason) and when he is onstage, I always experience a feeling of gratitude that, for once, a singer actually looks as romantic as he is supposed to look. In addition, he possesses an elemental, bronze voice and an animal vitality that never fail to excite me. When I hear Placido Domingo, it is his beauty of tone that moves me, also a musicianship and versatility that make him as satisfying in Ginastera's *Don Rodrigo* as in Verdi's *Don Carlo*. As for Jon Vickers, I admit the awesome physical impact of his presence, also the dramatic skill that makes his Otello and Peter Grimes so terrifying. But more than that, I enjoy listening to this huge, multicolored voice which makes me think of an iron column that weeps tears. I don't need to look at him; I hear everything in his voice.

I wish I were able to link these great tenors of the present with those of the past by relating how, in childhood, my life was shaken apart by a first hearing of Caruso, Martinelli, maybe Bjoerling. But trying to recall my first tenor, or even my first opera, is as impossible as trying to remember my first cup of coffee or my first summer day. Opera was always with me, but I'm afraid it didn't impress me very much when I was young and supposedly impressionable. Pianos, and the people who could play them, were what really excited me. The way a tenor could bawl up to a high C seemed to me a matter of talent, not skill, but the ability of a pianist to get only five fingers through the intricacies of a double-note scale without fracturing them all left me endlessly amazed.

As I grew older, though, and heard more singers, I came to realize that great singing is very much a matter of skill, even more than great playing. After all, if a pianist has a weak technique, he seldom wrecks his hands and absolutely never destroys his instrument. Careless singing, though, can reduce the most golden voice to a tinny travesty of its former self. When I learned this, my respect for singers soared. Today, I still care deeply about keyboard artists, but it is the unfortunate men and women whose lives are lived in willing slavery to their vocal cords who have earned my greatest admiration and my deepest pity.

Pity aside, I am enormously grateful to these five great tenors for enriching my life with their ability to make such wondrous noises. I further admire them for learning to perfect their gifts. Most of all, I am impressed with their mentalities, their willingness to channel their achievements into purely artistic directions.

As an editor, I am also impressed and grateful that they so cheerfully tolerated the questions and intrusions necessary to the writing of this book. The five men suffered being interrupted at mealtime, stared at during rehearsals, trailed into automobiles and airplanes, forced to gossip when they ought to have been saving their voices for more important matters, and in general had their lives disrupted. Now that it is all over, I hope they feel the results have been worth it. I do.

—HERBERT H. BRESLIN

# Richard Tucker

BY

*William Bender*

EVERY *day, it seems, there is a new refugee uncle or aunt from Rumania or Russia for whom room must be made in the tenement apartments, and more water added to the soup. . . . The streets tumble with children, merchants, carts, boxes, animals. . . . There is a mood for every face: sorrow, pride, hunger, ecstasy, fervor, grief, joy. . . .*

*The scene is the Lower East Side of New York in the early 1920s. . . . The time is three o'clock on any afternoon of the week in the Jewish ghetto, and at P.S. 64 on East 4th Street, school is out. . . . A boy darts around a corner and up the stairs where his mother is waiting with his favorite snack, a piece of bread spread with* shmaltz *(chicken fat). . . . Then down the stairs again for a half hour or so of baseball in the streets. . . . Then, two hours of Hebrew School. . . . Ah, the Saturday afternoons, standing outside*

*the Metro Music Company on Second Avenue, listen-
ing to the new recordings of Caruso and Chaliapin on the
store's sidewalk loudspeaker. . . . On Sunday, family song
sessions at home. . . . And three times a week, singing lessons
with Cantor Samuel Weiser who tells the boy that when he,
too, becomes a cantor someday, people will always want to
hear a beautiful voice. . . .*

The owner of the brick and white clapboard house in Great
Neck, New York, could afford a swimming pool if he so
desired. No need. Only a few minutes' drive away is one
of the comfortable beaches that has made the North Shore of
Long Island such a choice, and crowded, Manhattan suburban area. The house is basic early 1950s ranch, with a two-
story wing added on to provide bedrooms for the three sons
of the family who are now grown up, gone, but always
welcome back. The rugs are the softest money can buy, the
chairs the deepest. One of the ten rooms is a den, the walls
of which are covered with pictures of the master of the house
at work. Out back is a rolling garden where the owner and
his wife like to throw parties in the summer for two hundred
people at a clip. "I love people," he says, "and when I do a
thing, I like to do it big."

In the garage is a four-door, cranberry red Cadillac limousine, and every day, when the owner is not out of town, a
chauffeur named Lionel arrives at 9 A.M. to drive his boss to
work. The car ambles over curving lanes, through a maze of
green lawns and hedges, then aims for the Long Island Ex-
pressway and the trip to Manhattan gets seriously under
way. Driving in from the airport on a New York visit in
*Live and Let Die,* and taking many of the same routes,
Secret Agent James Bond would marvel at the sexual over-
tones of the road signs—"Soft Shoulders," "Squeeze," "Yield,"

"Merge," "Maintain Speed." Not this man. He is fondling his morning copy of *The New York Times* and is immersed in the sports pages and Wall Street report. Arriving at his *pied-à-terre*, a three-room apartment on Central Park South from which most of his business ventures are launched, he finds his schedule crammed with work sessions, interviews, a meeting with his manager, a meeting with his publicist. There will be expected phone calls from his stockbroker, unexpected calls from old friends and cronies who must see him that day. "What a life, what a life," he cries out at last. "People would think I was a bank president."

So they might. Indeed, there are any number of bank presidents throughout the United States who would envy his accumulated wealth and quarter-of-a-million-dollar income a year. This man is Richard Tucker, who did indeed grow up to be a cantor and did indeed develop a beautiful

Richard Tucker at home (*Photo by Erika Davidson*)

voice. Today he is best known as that rarest of breeds, an operatic tenor, a man who has built a fabulous career and a marvelous life on a freak of nature, two slender vocal cords that produce one sound in a million and that have steadfastly refused to grow old. It is no freak, or accident, though, that Tucker has set one record after another for longevity in a field in which the norm is sudden starburst and then fall-out. In matters vocal, he is a supreme craftsman. To Tucker, his clear, vibrant tenor voice is "God's gift," and, being deeply religious, he has exercised it, nurtured it, and protected it in the same way he would sanctify anything bestowed by the Almighty. At the Metropolitan Opera, which Tucker joined as a leading tenor in January 1945, it was Rudolf Bing who remarked early on during his reign as general manager: "Caruso, Caruso, that's all you hear. I have an idea we're going to be proud someday to be able to tell people we heard Tucker." Bing was right, of course, as he often was in matters dealing with divas and divos. Against all odds, Tucker has survived at the Met to the grand, old (operatically speaking) age of sixty, and with his vocal powers sturdily intact. His dozen or so performances of the romantic hero Gabriele in Verdi's *Simon Boccanegra* during the Met's 1973–1974 season were astonishing in their vocal security and command of the Italian style. The fall of 1974 brings with it the start of Tucker's thirtieth season at the Met—a record surpassed among tenors only by Giovanni Martinelli, who lasted thirty-two seasons.

Tucker is such an institution, in fact, that he is too often taken for granted. It is easy to disparage his bulky, somewhat squat, unromantic figure, not to mention his simplistic, often semaphoric acting. There are a few too many sobs in his old-school Italian singing style. Combined with that is the occasional grunt to punctuate a dramatic line, or the

all-too-infrequent pianissimo, or the top tones that sometimes linger on well past the conductor's cutoff.

Standing a mere five-foot-seven, paunchy and bald
(though never without a stylish black hairpiece), Tucker at
sixty is definitely no matron's dream of Prince Charming.
But expertly girdled and costumed, and also because of the
natural confidence he shares with all great singers, Tucker
comes off as a credible enough operatic lover—especially
when partnered in the past by a Milanov or Albanese, and
now by a Caballé or Maliponte. He may not bother with
scholarly research into the backgrounds of his roles, but he
is invariably a thoroughly prepared master of the musical
styles involved. Technically, he knows what he is doing
every minute of the time, and it is this technical knowledge
that enables him to surmount any inroads on his vocal
equipment made by the advancing years. The voice itself
has a clear, precise, easily recognizable clarion quality. The
free tone production and the undeniable dramatic intensity
of Tucker's delivery can be breathtaking at times. If Tucker
is not, as his fans insist, singing better today than ever, he is
certainly singing every bit as well.

Tucker remains one of the true standard-bearers of the
Italian operatic tradition. That is a remarkable accomplishment for a man who is, after all, an American, born in
Brooklyn of Rumanian immigrant parents, who has had all
his musical training in the United States from teachers of
non-Italian affiliation. Paul Althouse, his principal voice
teacher, was an American from Pennsylvania best known for
Wagnerian roles at the Met. Joseph Garnett, who has
coached Tucker in every one of his parts, is a Pole, German-
educated, who served as an assistant to Fritz Busch at the
Dresden State Opera before coming to America. How is this
possible? Tucker himself attributes his vocal flexibility to

his early studies of *chazanuth*, the Hebrew liturgy intoned by synagogue cantors.

Tucker began that training by joining a synagogue choir at age six. He had been born on August 28, 1913, the son of an immigrant Rumanian furrier, and the baby of a family that included one other boy and three girls. The family's first home was a flat in the Brownsville section of Brooklyn. Shortly after Richard's birth, they moved to the Lower East Side of Manhattan and a walk-up on 4th Street between First and Second Avenues. "It was a real Jewish ghetto," recalls Tucker, "but the Jews were proud and they worked hard." Tucker has no regrets about his childhood, and all things considered, it was a reasonably happy life. Poppa Samuel loved music, and every Sunday there was a songfest in the Tucker house with relatives and friends crowded in. "It was just like Sam Levenson described it in one of his stories," says Tucker. "If more people came than we expected, momma would just add a little water to the soup. Momma was always finding pennies from heaven, and somehow there was always enough meat in the pot."

Even as a boy, Richard always carried his end of the singing load, and so it was understandable he should be sent to Cantor Samuel Weiser to learn to be a cantor. "He took to me like a son," recalls Tucker, in words markedly similar to those he would use in describing his first lessons, years later, with Paul Althouse. Richard was one of those rare children who could not only carry a tune, but could also harmonize accurately and dependably. Cantor Weiser immediately began grooming him to become leader of the choir's second soprano section. Richard's starting salary was $25 a year. By the time his voice changed at age fourteen, he was making $150. "It was not so much the money, but being proud to be a member of the choir," he says.

Tucker admits that he was not much of a success as a

choirboy his first year. "I stood there for a year practically, listening." Small wonder. The youngest choirboys were usually seven or eight. His mother had pushed him into it a year early, just as she had finagled him into first grade in public school at age five. "You know how mothers are," he says, "they lie about the age." The thirty boys in the choir wore black gowns and skullcaps, learned to sight read their hymns, chants, and responses, and sang everything in Hebrew.

It was a strict routine. In addition to rehearsals during the week, the Sabbath involved an hour-and-a-half service on Friday night, and another service three hours long on Saturday morning. The High Holy Days meant longer services, including the Day of Atonement from sundown to sundown. The small boys in the choir, Richard included, were allowed to run home at noon for lunch on that day, but after the age of bar mitzvah (thirteen), they had to fast like the men. Tucker remembers how every Friday at noon, his father Samuel would close his shop and retire to a Turkish bath "to be cleansed for the Sabbath. He always sat on the top step at the bath because he loved the steam so much." In the days when his sons were coming of age, it used to sadden Tucker that the old ways exercised less pull on his family. None of his sons sang in the temple at Great Neck. In fact, he told an interviewer in 1952, "Nowadays, kids tell their parents, 'I don't want to go'—to the temple, even. Sing in the choir? That died with my mother."

Tucker meanwhile was moving ahead nicely in school. "I was always in the R. A.'s"—rapid advance classes in which two terms' work was done in one. "Still," he says, "I always wanted to be a businessman," and he quit school at fifteen and took a job as a Wall Street runner. By then he had already changed his name from Reuben Ticker. His employers were two Irishmen, Kelly and Shannon, who liked the youngster enough to persuade him to go back to what was then known as continuation school. And so, for another year he went to school in the mornings and worked for Kelly and Shannon in the afternoons. At the start, his duties consisted mostly of errands, such as delivering stocks to brokers' offices. Since he was carrying valuable securities, he was bonded, and once he delivered nearly $1,000,000 in checks to the floor of the stock exchange. Those were days just before the 1929 crash. Tucker was making $20 a week.

He says he speculated only once during that period. He and another runner pooled their savings and bought some stock selling for $4 a share. It closed that same day at $6, and Tucker went home delirious. "The next morning, when the exchange opened, the stock was selling at $5." That he could lose money overnight, when no business was being done, baffled him. He sold, took his $1 profit, and never invested in stocks again until almost twenty-five years later. He was on the floor the day of the crash, and, at a tender age, knew instinctively that one phase of his life was over.

At Cantor Weiser's insistence, Tucker did no singing at all between the ages of fourteen and seventeen. That was to protect his budding tenor voice during a period of growth and maturation. At eighteen, Weiser gave him the green light. "Singing again, testing out the notes, I was like a young colt," recalls Tucker. Until the age of twenty-one, he was a regular tenor in the choir, and four nights a week he studied the cantorial arts comprehensively under Weiser. He sang for nothing in the choir to pay for his lessons.

It was not long before Tucker moved out on his own. He got his first job as a cantor—three High Holy Days at Beth Madrish Hagodal in the Washington Heights section of Upper Manhattan—by answering an advertisement in a newspaper. There is, of course, much more decorum involved in the hiring of a cantor these days. His first permanent cantor's job was at Temple Emanuel in Passaic, New Jersey. From there he moved to Temple Adeth Israel in the Bronx. Tucker's training had, of course, been Orthodox, but this was a Conservative synagogue, and his first experience with organ accompaniment. From the cantor's point of view, recalls Tucker, "you can elaborate more in the Conservative." The Orthodox was cut and dried: "You just sing and get out." The leader of the Adeth Israel choir was an organist named Zavel Zilberts, who composed choral music and gave an annual choral concert in Town Hall. Tucker made his concert debut with Zilberts in 1939 in Rossini's *Stabat Mater*, and there was considerable shaking of heads about the Adeth Israel cantor singing a stabat mater. In 1943 Tucker moved over to the Brooklyn Jewish Center, which, as far as he was concerned, was the St. Patrick's Cathedral of Conservative Judaism, and was still that congregation's cantor—on a sixty-day leave of absence—when he made his Met debut.

He did not quit the Brooklyn Jewish Center until the Met was a sure thing, but for years thereafter he went back regularly for the holidays. To this day, he keeps up his cantorial work at the holy days. "It's too much imbedded in me. I couldn't give it up." Over the years he has sung as cantor in many of America's major cities—Chicago, Milwaukee, Cleveland, Miami Beach, as well as New York—and by the early 1950s ranked as the highest paid cantor in the United States. His fee then was $10,000 for the three holy days. "When they pay $25 a ticket, you have to deliver. I give more in those three days than in ten operas." And fasting all the while, of course. To Tucker, there is no essential difference between cantorial and Italian operatic singing. "They both demand blood and guts."

Wall Street having of necessity changed its ways with the advent of the Depression, Tucker the businessman moved several miles uptown to the garment district. Again, he started out as an errand boy and this time worked his way up to part-time salesman waiting on customers. It was at this point that Sara Perelmuth, his bride-to-be, entered his life. Over the years, Tucker would grow fond of referring to Sara as "a simple girl, down to earth. She has her two feet on the ground, just what an artist needs." One Sunday during the winter of 1974, Sara came back from hearing pianist Arthur Rubinstein give a piano recital in Manhattan, and, with an obvious dig at her husband's predilection for TV sports on Sunday afternoons, said to him pointedly: "I'll tell you one thing, football he ain't got on his mind." Tucker chuckled about it later. "I just loved that crack, it really broke me up." Not too long ago, a business associate of the singer's was trying desperately to think of an unusual present to give him—by and large, Tucker has everything—and sounded Sara out about the possibility of a set of calling cards. "What does he need calling cards for?" asked Sara. "Everybody knows who Richard Tucker is."

In the 1930s, though, Tucker would tell her, "I'm just a budding rosebush, but I'm going to bud." And, says Sara, "God help us, he really did." They met one day when he was singing for a banquet at her parents' catering place known as Grand Mansion. One of Sara's uncles introduced them. Something clicked, but it was hardly love at first sight, more like a time-release cold capsule. The pill went off six months later when he blithely called her up to say hello. Then nothing for another six months, until one day a subway door opened at the Brighton Beach station, and there was Sara. "She had a terrific sunburn," he recalls, "and that was when Cupid hit me." Tucker was also hit by the fact that while he was making $25 a week, "she was a secretary, and making more than me—$26." They were married the

following winter, on February 11, 1936. Among those present was Sara's brother who was already making a name for
himself as a singer and would eventually become as well
known at the Met as Tucker—Jan Peerce.

Sara's mother evinced an immediate interest in Richard's
career by marching into WEVD, a Jewish-oriented radio
station in New York then owned by the magazine *Daily
Forward*, and getting him a job singing on a Sunday morn-
·ing program—some Jewish songs, some classical. Outside the
synagogues, says Tucker, "that was my first ten bucks from
singing." Meanwhile, with the combined savings of the bride
and bridegroom and the help of a small loan (total capital:
$4,500), Tucker set himself up in business as what is known
as a convertor. A convertor makes linings for fur coats, buy-
ing raw silk and dyeing it to order for furriers. The little
company flourished, and Tucker kept it going until 1949,
long after he had made it at the Met and established himself as a concert and recording artist.

In 1939 Tucker began studying with the Met's Wagnerian
tenor Paul Althouse. "When I went to see him the first
time," says Tucker, "it was like father and son." Along with
God, Sara, and Cantor Weiser, Tucker rightly considers
Althouse as one of the four most important influences in his
life. Frank St. Leger, then a Met conductor but soon to become right-hand man to General Manager Edward Johnson,
was to say later of Althouse's work with Tucker: "He took
the cantor tricks out." There was more to it than that, of
course. "How would you like to be met at the door and told
to forget there ever was a Caruso?" asks Tucker rhetorically.
Althouse, whose other pupils included Eleanor Steber, would
not let Tucker imitate any other singers, would not let him
force ("Let the others shout themselves hoarse, you're going
to survive"), would not let him touch a role until Althouse

considered him ready. "And this is something I've never revealed before," says Tucker. "Paul Althouse made me swear I would never sing a German vowel as long as I lived, and I haven't." When Althouse died in 1954, says Tucker, "he was listening to me on a Saturday afternoon broadcast of *Traviata*. He had never let anybody know he had cancer."

In an interview a few years before his death, Althouse recalled that when Tucker first set foot on an operatic stage—with New York's Salmaggi Opera Company—"he sang with one paralyzed arm and one broken arm in a sling." Althouse did not mean that literally, of course, that was his way of describing Tucker's stage posture—one arm hanging straight down, the other crooked at the elbow. "But he sang like an angel." Tucker stayed with Althouse right up until the latter's death, and his manner never changed at all during that period. As Althouse recalled it, Tucker would just come for his lesson, take his hat off, sing, put his hat back on, and leave. Most of the lessons were at Althouse's studio—half scaling, half polishing phrases—but occasionally Althouse would go down to the Met a half hour before performance and warm Tucker up in his dressing room. "Sometimes," said Althouse, "I'd put down a nickel and bet him he couldn't get through something without a mistake. He's that kind of guy."

Althouse's principal efforts were to give Tucker more confidence in his top tones, and more color. When he first started with Althouse, Tucker had only a high A-flat. Resorting to a favorite teacher's ruse, Althouse would hit an A on the piano and tell Tucker it was an A-flat. Tucker would try to match it, and in time, said Althouse, developed "a good solid C."

To Althouse, Tucker right at the start displayed "a very fine natural musicianship . . . an extraordinary concentration and memory. He memorizes very quickly. It's uncanny." Althouse knew that Tucker's voice would get heavier as the singer got older, but in the early years he tried to confine him to the lighter roles. "I try to keep him pointed toward the lyric, such as Mozart." That took some doing. Tucker has always been deferential to Mozart, rather than passionate. *Così fan Tutte,* which he has done at the Met off and on for years since the introduction of the Alfred Lunt production in 1952, he once described as "an opera that melts in the throat." And he conceded that Mozart's music was one of the fundamental beginnings of any singer. But, with his eye ever on the box office, Tucker did not want to specialize in that composer's music because he considered the Mozart public too small. "A Mozartean singer in this country has never made a success."

Althouse began talking about Tucker to his Met colleagues, and conductor Wilfred Pelletier soon came around to hear what all the talking was about. Pelletier told me, says Tucker, "that if I could keep on studying, I couldn't miss." And in 1942, with Pelletier's help, Tucker was enrolled as a contestant in the Metropolitan Auditions of the Air, sponsored by the Sherwin Williams paint company. Pelletier was a good man to know. As the Met's man in charge of the auditions, he heard 800 to 900 voices a year, then arranged for coaches to help the most promising youngsters. Tucker went on and, much to his chagrin, finished among the semifinalists. He never again competed in the contest, but it did not really matter. The Met had liked what it heard, and in 1944 he was given an audition on the main stage of the house with, as usual, a single light bulb burning, and, not so usual, General Manager Edward Johnson, his assistant, Frank St. Leger, and conductor Emil Cooper sitting out in the darkened hall. When Tucker had finished singing, a voice came floating up to the stage: "I will assume full responsibility for this man's career." It was Cooper's.

Tucker recalls that Johnson, who had done some free-lancing in synagogues himself, told him later: "If you can satisfy 1,500 people in a temple with your singing, I have no fear that you can satisfy 4,000 at the Met." Nonetheless, the first offer put to Tucker by St. Leger was the Italian singer in act one of *Der Rosenkavalier*. Tucker declined, with the cocksure attitude that was already hardening firmly in his character. "I said to St. Leger, 'If I come in, I come in through the front door. I want a major role.' I've always followed that policy, and thank God, it's always been lucky. Some people go out of town to try out. Not me. With me, it was always a king or a bum. That's the way it is with me."

And so, on January 25, 1945, Tucker strode out onto the Met stage for the first time, an American with no European operatic experience at all, and precious little time in the opera houses of his native land to boot. The opera was Ponchielli's *La Gioconda*, which the Met was mounting for the first time since the 1939–40 season. It was one of the dazzling casts the Met could assemble almost routinely in those days. Singing the title role for the first time opposite Tucker's Enzo was Stella Roman. In the role of Laura was Bruna Castagna; Margaret Harshaw was La Cieca. The Alvise was Nicola Moscona, and the Barnaba, Richard Bonelli. On the podium was Cooper. Tucker impressed the audience, and the Met brass. "Right away he had turned the point," recalled Pelletier. "He was not an amateur."

In general, the reviews were hugely favorable, although Noel Strauss in *The New York Times* did not find the role too well suited for the singer:

"Special interest naturally centered in the company's new tenor, Mr. Tucker, who had the misfortune to make his

initial appearance in a formidable role too heavy for his
essentially lyric type of voice. Nevertheless, he made a
definitely favorable impression and was enthusiastically received by the large audience. Although inexperienced in
opera, he sang Enzo's music with poise and assurance. His
tones were steady and of pleasing quality, boasting special
richness and resonance above the staff, where the sounds
produced were more 'forward' than in the thinner lower
half of the scale. He sang with warmth and expressiveness
and his acting was natural and easy. Besides these virtues he
had an agreeable stage presence. But he must be heard in a
part more congenial to him before final judgment can be
made of his capabilities."

In the *New York Herald Tribune*, Virgil Thomson wrote:
"Mr. Tucker is an Italian-style tenor of middle-sized voice,
rather like that of Jan Peerce, his cousin [*sic*]. He should be
useful because his work is mostly sound and occasionally
quite beautiful, especially the loud high notes. He sings well
forward as to facial resonance and right on pitch." In the
*Telegram* Robert Bagar noted that Tucker had a pleasant
voice, sang intelligently, and phrased musically, "But he
wants volume of voice for a role like Enzo and—even more
than volume—he wants impact . . . not a dramatic voice . . .
isn't even a spinto, except here and there . . . hasn't the true
dramatic tenor's ping, or the body, yet it is a voice of liquid
quality . . . more suitable for lighter parts." Reviewing a
subsequent *Gioconda*, the *Musical Courier* reported that
"the new tenor, in voice and appearance, brought to mind
the vanished Golden Era of Opera." The *Courier* also noted,
without naming any names, that at one point someone
stepped on Roman's train. She "was badly shaken and cut
both her knees. While the half-dazed soprano clung to members of the cast in the 3rd act . . . the tenor rose to his best

heights of song. She too carried on vocally, but not without glaring more or less murderously at the rest of the cast."

Over the next few years, as Tucker went on to add *La Bohème, Madama Butterfly, Manon Lescaut, Lucia di Lammermoor,* and *Un Ballo in Maschera* to his repertory, he provoked the same kind of critical split. In 1946, the usually tart-tongued Claudia Cassidy of the *Chicago Tribune* would say, "His voice has that rarest of natural gifts, a beautiful quality of tone." And in 1949, Irving Kolodin in *Saturday Review* would remark after a *Manon Lescaut*: ". . . another part in which he manifests his rapid ascension to rank not only as a leading tenor but 'the' leading tenor of the company." Still, in 1947 the *Times* would report that "[He] played the part of [Rodolfo] with all the reckless abandon of a bank president . . . most of his posturing was as absurd as the kiss he blew to the audience as it applauded his vocal accomplishments after the third act." And in 1951, Louis Biancolli in the *World-Telegram* wrote: "Tucker once more demonstrated that if he continues singing as beautifully as he does, a new Mario Lanza will be signed up by Hollywood some day to do 'The Great Tucker.' What a voice!"

Tucker was tickled by Biancolli's appraisal—and would cite it to interviewers for years thereafter—and it helped him shake off any doubts about himself. "Regardless of the critics' attacking my stage presence, they could never attack my voice," he says. True enough. Nonetheless, the needling about his acting did on one occasion become more than he could stand, and he fired off a telegram to Harold C. Schonberg of the *Times*. It read in its entirety: "Drop dead."

Tucker meanwhile was keeping his free-lance options open. In 1944 he had started singing on the radio program "Chicago Theater of the Air," originating at Chicago's station WGN. For the next six or seven years, he commuted to Chicago by plane every Saturday (unless he had a Met engagement) and sang arias in English from operas like *Bohème, Traviata,* and *Faust,* and from operettas like *The Student Prince* and *Vagabond King.* The high point of those days, however, was the 1947 broadcast of *Aïda* with Toscanini from Studio 8-H in Manhattan's RCA Building. It had long been Tucker's—and Sara's—dream that he would some day sing for The Maestro. "We wouldn't have cared if he didn't take me, just to have him hear me was all we wanted. It would be a niche in my career." When he got to 8-H, there were only a handful of people there: Toscanini and his son Walter, Tucker and Sara, and his accompanist, Joseph Garnett. "Maestro says, 'Do you know *Aïda?*' I says, 'No, maestro.' He says, 'Why don't you sing it?' I says, 'It's too heavy, but for you, for radio . . .' He says, 'But you sing *Gioconda* so well.'" At this, Tucker was amazed, not expecting Toscanini ever to have heard him sing. "People think in their lives nothing is noticed." Then Toscanini asked him to sing "Celeste Aïda," and when he finished, Toscanini said 'Bravo,' and he was hired.

For the next four weeks Tucker gave up all outside engagements and worked with his coach—Garnett. In one of the later rehearsals, with all the principals present, Tucker got into the *Celeste* aria. Toscanini halted the rehearsal and asked:

"Do you love a woman, Tucker?"

Tucker was flustered—"The women all around, how could I say, I was embarrassed."

Toscanini repeated the question exactly.

"Yes," said Tucker finally.

"Well, show it. *CELESTIAL* Aïda. You're so morbid and sad. Is it *me?*"

"But what tenor sings it smiling?"

Richard Tucker as Radames in Verdi's *Aïda* (*Photo by Louis Mélançon*)

"No one. You're going to be the first one."

In the last act, when Radames discovers that Aïda has sneaked into the dungeon to die with him, Toscanini again stopped the music. "Why aren't you happy?"

"Maestro, I'm *not* happy, I'm dying."

"You *are* happy. She has sacrificed her life, you are dying with the woman you love, you're *happy*."

Working with Toscanini was probably one of the happiest things that happened to Tucker. "At the end of the performance I was in a different world." To this day, Toscanini's autographed picture is the only one in Tucker's den of any musician besides himself.

Tucker had been considerably buoyed for his appearance with Toscanini by a summer trip to Italy the year before, where he made his Italian debut in Verona, again in *Gioconda*. Afterward, Sara noted a "marked change" in both her husband's performing and personal confidence. As Tucker himself remarked later, "It gave me an approach. The Italian people showed us what opera really means, in understanding and appreciating an artist. You feel different because you sense the people know what the hell you're doing, like a ballplayer in the big leagues knows there are people in the stands who know baseball."

There was a moment, though, when he thought the people were going to come down out of the stands and onto the ball field. Tucker was tired after his winter work, and in the dress rehearsal, he sang falsetto to rest his voice. Unknown to Tucker, everybody comes to the rehearsal in Verona. When he began to sing softly, there was a commotion out front. The conductor, Tullio Serafin, explained to him that people didn't know whether he could sing or not; his records were not then available in Italy. So when it came to the aria *Cielo e mar*, he sang full voice. "This mass threw themselves on the stage and started to kiss me." At the performance, it was a somewhat different story. In Verona candles are sold outside the Arena, and once inside, the audience lights up to indicate appreciation. There were about 2,500 in the audience, and during one aria, they began to light their candles. Tucker was stunned: "All of a sudden I'm standing before a candelabra. I didn't know what it was. Then when I finished, there was such a tumultuous shout, not applause, a shouting. *Bis! Bis!* [Encore] I thought they're calling me a beast." He got through the opera and went to his dressing room, where his wife was waiting. All he could say was, "Sara, what happened?" What had happened, of course, was that he had scored a huge personal triumph.

At this point in his career, it became apparent that two traits, among others, would be forever imbedded in his character and professional style. One was the fact that he would never ambitiously pursue an international career. Thoughts of home and family would pop up regularly in his conversations and in public utterances. It seemed that he could not get through three sentences without saying "my wife and I figured out" or "as I tell my boys" or "when I get home" or "as I left home" or "I couldn't leave home just then." He was a man immensely and obviously proud of his wife, his boys, his home, and, sometimes to an embarrassing degree, himself. He never actually went so far as to say that he was the greatest tenor in the world, but he never hesitated to mention many powerful operatic figures who did say so. In talking about a role like Canio in *Pagliacci*, for instance, he once remarked without so much as a blink: "Of course I can sing it better than anyone else, there isn't another tenor in the world who can equal me just singing it. . . ."

Richard Tucker with his wife and sons (*left to right*) David, Richard Tucker, Sara, Barry and Henry (*Photo by Bob Serating, Courtesy of Lincoln Center for the Performing Arts*)

The second trait was that he was never going to forget his Jewish heritage—or idly mimic any other religion. "The mother of opera is Italy and all of it has to do with the church," he declared. "I never like to desecrate any religion." Regardless of Verdi's many requests, Tucker would not wear a cross. "A cross is a symbol of faith, like the star is a symbol of our faith." In *Boris Godunov,* for instance, as the Pretender Dmitri, Tucker normally would have worn a jeweled chain around his neck with a cross on it; instead he wore a large brass emblem, signifying nothing. When he had to be blessed, he was blessed not with the gesture of the cross but "just with the two hands." He also began turning down certain concert dates for religious reasons, say, a part in Berlioz's *L'Enfance du Christ.*

Tucker went to the Met in 1945 for $250 a week. By the time Bing arrived on the scene in 1951, says Tucker, "I was singing for $350 a week. When I went in to sign my new contract, and I was the first singer, the very first singer in this house asked to sign that season, I asked for $750 a performance. Bing just looked at me, then offered me $650. Now, I knew he was going to use me twice a week and that meant a lot of difference. Finally I asked him if he was a gambler. He never took his eyes off me, nodded yes. All right, I said, my personal representative, Thea Dispeker, who was with me, would toss a coin. He could call and I'd abide by the fall. He did and he won and it cost me $2,000 that year because of the toss! I talked to my wife about it, but she didn't care, she always wanted me to take it easy. . . ." And besides, "Edward Johnson, he brought me up, but Mr. Bing put me over the top," said Tucker in the early 1950s. "Johnson and St. Leger made me. They picked me up off the street and in five years they built me a repertory. I wouldn't for the world say a thing against them. But it is a happier house now. Look at that chorus, those clothes. Why those girls . . . you know, they know they look good, so they try to sing real good, better than ever."

Bing became as fond of Tucker as any of his singers, largely because, for all his cocksureness, he was not the usual flighty type of whom Bing said at the time: "They think because they are rare that they can hold you up, that you cannot get along without them and so they want to show you. If you have a contract with a fixed fee, then they pull a tantrum or walk off the stage, just to show you that they are necessary to you. 'Temperament!' Bloody-mindedness, that's all it is." But not Tucker. "He's no actor, though Tyrone Guthrie, who is a really great stage director, discovered that if you simply gave Tucker something to hold onto, he was all right on stage and that his voice would do the rest. And it is true. He sings so feelingly, so sensuously

that he can be very moving, very vivid. He throws himself
so vocally into a role that his acting limitations are seldom
serious. He looks very much just what he is, a man you
could meet out there on Seventh Avenue a few blocks south,
and I guess that is where he came from. But in his voice is
everything. You know, of course, that I did not bring Tucker
to this house. He was here when I came. But I think I have
been able to help Tucker, and I think he will agree with
this. When I came here he was a more or less minor singer
in this house. But by bringing him forward and giving him
first nights and that kind of thing, I think I have helped him
find himself."

That did not stop Bing from writing to *Life* magazine,
after its publication in 1952 of a highly favorable article
('Pagliacci from Brooklyn,' LIFE, November 3) on Tucker
by Winthrop Sargeant (later to switch over to *The New
Yorker*). Bing's note read: "Will you permit me a small
correction in the article on Mr. Richard Tucker? There was
a sentence which read, 'Already he is singing 20 roles with
passion and extraordinary endurance, and Rudolf Bing, the
Met's general arranger, has given [him] his choice of the
best roles of the season.'

"While I do not in any way wish to belittle Mr. Tucker's
outstanding qualities, I cannot accept the statement that he
chooses his own parts or has a position that differs from his
most excellent colleagues because it simply is not so."

That phased Tucker not at all. "He's the boss. He knows
it and he makes everyone know it. And yet, funny, but he
can walk down the aisle and no one would take him for the
general manager. . . . It's his enthusiasm that has caught on.
He watches everything. He's all over the place all the time,
and he's enthusiastic about what we're doing. That makes a
difference, you know."

Bing even managed to sell Tucker on the role of Ferrando in *Così fan Tutte*. "He told me he'd like me to sing it, and when I looked at the part, I said why it's a small role, that's for a second tenor. But he said to me, 'Mr. Tucker, I want you to sing that role. The greatest tenors in Europe sing it all the time. It is a very important role.' And it is. He knew I was right for that role."

Introduced at Christmastime during Bing's first season, *Così* was done up in stylized rococo settings designed by Rolf Gérard, sung in English, and presided over by the Broadway actor and director Alfred Lunt, who entered into the operatic festivities himself by appearing before the footlights as a mute servant lighting the lamps and otherwise presiding over the evening's goings-on. The whole thing was somewhat overblown, but Eleanor Steber sang an unforgettable Fiordiligi, and the others in the cast were admirable. Blanche Thebom as Dorabella, Patrice Munsel as Despina, Frank Guarrera as Guglielmo, and John Brownlee as Don Alfonso. Fritz Stiedry conducted. Writing in the *Times* the next day, Olin Downes remarked of the leading tenor: "Mr. Tucker's magnificent voice was greatly enjoyed, though he erred on the sentimental side."

Sentimental Tucker may have been, but what would he have been like, especially in such a heady, rarefied stylistic atmosphere, if Lunt had not worked so hard with the singer at rehearsals? Said Tucker to Lunt at the first one: "I'm the worst actor you ever saw." Replied Lunt to Tucker: "I don't believe it and I don't think you should believe it." They had met on the way to a gathering of the cast to break the ice for Lunt. "He was sitting profile in the taxi," Lunt recalled. "I told him he looked exactly like Louis the Fourteenth, even that chin. He does, you know, really." Later, Lynn Fontanne told Lunt, "He has beautiful eyes and

a sweet sensitive face. Tell him. Tell him." Lunt did. "He
brushed it away."

At that first rehearsal, Tucker cried out: "Wait a minute,
let's read the words before we sing so we'll know what we're
talking about." "There you are," observed Lunt later, "that's
the essence of an actor." Lunt coaxed, encouraged, and even
tried to flatter Tucker into good acting. He would say: "Your
voice is Venetian velvet, which you have disciplined for
years and years and years. You can do the same with your
acting. It's like the man who was asked whether he played
the violin. He said, 'I don't know. I've never tried.' You have
all the sadness of your race and you couldn't go around Eli,
Eli, Eli-ing without having knowledge of sorrow."

Lunt confided to an interviewer, "Of course he is not
developed as an actor, but he feels his costume, he's
very quick on his feet, he moves with great rapidity. He's
sensitive about his height, but without reason." At the end
of the first act Tucker did a tricky little dance step that
Lunt found "quite good really, it has to be timed beautifully." Lunt even took two of Tucker's suggestions at rehearsals. The first was when he was singing Ferrando's
laughing song. Tucker began to wave his hat back and
forth; Lunt liked it and told him to leave it in. The second
was during the snuff-taking scene; Tucker proposed taking
it not from his own pocket, but from Don Alfonso's. This too
Lunt left in.

Tucker did not lack for fine directors. Tyrone Guthrie,
who guided Tucker in *Carmen,* once interrupted a complaint
session about the general level of acting at the Met to say
of the Don José, "But Tucker has a quite beautiful face, you
know. Beautiful planes." And remarkably fine facial skin,
almost pearly and with a warm pink glow showing above
the blue chin and jowls. Even in middle age, his cheeks

remain flat and smooth, the nose finely molded and straight, the dark eyes well set under a broad, clear brow.

Whatever the director may have thought, Tucker says that after his experience with Guthrie he found dramatic and romantic roles much easier going. Referring to "this business of acting," Tucker says "I never really understood what they were talking about, what was wrong, what would be right if I just 'loosened up and didn't act like a stick.' And then Mr. Guthrie came along, this great director, a famous director, and he walked into the first rehearsal, threw off his coat and his tie, rolled up his sleeve, and said, 'Well, let's get this goddamned show on the road.' I don't know . . . I guess that loosened me up." In time, Tucker would come to regard Des Grieux in *Manon Lescaut* as his favorite role. "It's about love and love is easy to sing about. It's warm and human. Puccini, there's my man. I like Verdi, too, but Puccini is my favorite."

So infatuated with Puccini in fact that it seemed he was beginning to see himself as a real-life Rodolfo, who sings out in *Bohème* "Who am I?—I am a poet. . . . In poverty yet I indulge myself like a grand seigneur in rhymes . . ." Translation: Tucker had been amusing himself backstage spouting doggerel, some of which found its way into *Time* in the April 21, 1952 issue.

> Dear Mimi, sweet Mimi
> Of *La Bohème* fame.
> Face, pretty as a picture,
> And gosh! What a frame!
>
> Carmen could be charmin',
> Knittin' and darnin',
> But we prefer, most of us guys,
> A Carmen who's pulling the wool over our eyes.

Poor disappointed Don Carlo
Wanting a Queen for his doll-o,
Found that his midnight visitor
Was only the Grand Inquisitor.

And one for the boss:

Ode to Rudolf Bing
"For he I sing!"

Tucker also began to feel that there was a certain divinity in the stature and place of any great singer, himself included. "You know," he once said, "I think some people are messengers, and I think I'm one of them." Accordingly, he signed a fairly eloquent little essay in which he argued that truthfulness was the key to spiritual happiness. It was first heard, read by Tucker himself, on one of Edward R. Murrow's radio programs. Subsequently, it was printed in the *New York Herald Tribune* on March 23, 1953. It is worth quoting in full:

Spiritual happiness is to make peace with yourself, your neighbor and with God. And honesty has always been, for me, the grounds on which my Maker, my fellow men, and I meet as friends. Therefore, honesty is synonymous with spiritual happiness in my life.

People complain that so much sadness and loneliness exist today because of the complexity of the world. Some reasons for complexity are lies, half-truths, evasions—all of which inevitably result in confusion.

I have found that the way out of any confusing situation is to tell the truth. And there must be a strict definition of what is truth.

My youngest son once asked me, "What's so terrible about a little white lie?"

I said, "What do you mean by a white lie?"

"One that doesn't hurt anybody."

"Are you somebody?" I asked.

"Of course!" He was indignant.

"Then you are hurting someone with a white lie—yourself," I answered. "By lying you're accustoming yourself to a way of life that has neither integrity nor meaning. It adds you to the millions who face their neighbors with suspicion. The 'you show me and maybe I'll believe you' attitude so popular today comes from too much lying. For true brotherhood to exist there must be confidence in your fellow man and confidence is built on a conviction that your brother human being is telling the truth."

I tried to point out to my son that he hurt himself by any lie, and that from a larger viewpoint, he hurt the world. I think he understood.

And I hope that, beyond this, he realized that in believing in honesty for himself and for others, he also put faith in living with a certain amount of courage—because telling the truth is often not easy. To me truth implies that I am willing to face the consequences of my acts. Certainly there are many immediate embarrassments I could get out of by lying. But, in doing so, I would have evaded the mistake that made the lie necessary.

It is better to give myself some definition—to have the situation in my control, rather than let the situation control me. In lying I would be admitting that the problem is too big for me, and I must avoid it through a lie. But if I believe that the essential wonder of man is his ability to reckon with his environment, I will know that telling the truth means that I am afraid of pitting myself against any problem.

And not the least of the benefits of honesty is the comfort that comes to me in trouble, when I can think, "At least I've told the truth."

For all these reasons, I pray in the words George Washington used in a letter to Alexander Hamilton—"I hope I shall always possess firmness and virtue enough to maintain (what I consider the most enviable of all titles) the character of an honest man."

Richard Tucker as Canio in Leoncavallo's *I Pagliacci* (*Photo by Frank Dunand/Metropolitan Opera Guild*)

By then, Tucker was a staple on Columbia Records' vocal roster. He had made several cantorial LPs, and participated in many of the company's recordings of the Met—such as *Così, Lucia, Bohème,* and *Pagliacci* (the first three of which have recently been reissued on Columbia's Odyssey label). The issuance of the *Pagliacci* found Tucker in typical self-promotional form: "My greatest thing to date," he told one interviewer. "When I heard it, I couldn't believe it. I don't know whether I was man or beast that day." Man or beast! Even at his most immodest moments, Tucker could always manage to induce a chuckle in anybody. And what was one to make of his press agent's planting an item in a gossip column to the effect that a new ten-year contract with Columbia had been recorded on an unbreakable disc. "Lawyers now are wondering whether this constitutes an oral contract or a written one." Oh, boy!

One of Tucker's mentors at the time, by virtue of the Columbia contract, was Goddard Lieberson, eventually to become president of the company, but then its director of classical records. Lieberson found Tucker dependable and a fine singer, but apparently did not always know what to make of his charge. "He's not an American tenor," said Lieberson, "he's a New York tenor. He brings the Seventh Avenue [garment district] level to discussions of art, and, of course, it's funny, unintentionally." To Lieberson, Tucker's interests were mainly business. "He thinks of himself as a commodity. He's very sharp about extorting the last possible penny." Asked if Tucker's agent, Thea Dispeker, did not handle the negotiations, Lieberson replied with an obvious mixture of respect, awe, and pain: "She does it, but he always comes in for the kill."

Tucker began visiting California—where, from time to time, he would "rescue" the Hollywood Bowl—and dropping by the movie studios where he knew dickering was going on with Caruso's widow for the screen rights to the Caruso story. To no avail. MGM signed Mario Lanza. Said Tucker later to a reporter: "Did you see that thing Louis Biancolli wrote about me—you should get it, it's a good copy—something like next they ought to have Mario Lanza in *The Great Tucker*." Something like that.

At this point in the story of Richard Tucker, it becomes necessary to place the singer's egocentricity in its proper perspective. Tucker does come on a bit strong the first time one meets him, or encounters his boastful pronouncements. Yet there is something of the true *naïf* about him. At the center of his world is the simple, enduring, operative premise that God gave it to him to be the world's greatest tenor. Everything else—the furtherance of the career, his opinion on what music is suitable for the voice, his confidence in himself—everything revolves about that notion. Once one accepts it, one finds that Tucker is, as few other tenors, immensely humble in the face of his talent. He is also an incredibly loyal and generous person. An old friend from the garment district can always come around and, if on hard times, put the touch on Tucker for $20. When the husband of his latest press agent, Alix Williamson, was sick a few years ago, Tucker was on tour but rose early each morning to go to a synagogue and say a prayer. Then he would call Alix by phone each day to ask how Joe (Lippman, of the Herbert Barrett Management office) was. Joseph Garnett, a Polish Jew who worked in opera in Dresden before World War II and who coached Elisabeth Rethberg and Nelson Eddy, is a man Tucker met in 1941 at WEVD. That he should ever do without Garnett as coach and recital accompanist has never occurred to Tucker. Met Baritone Frank Guarrera recalls that during a rehearsal on the roof stage of the old Met, he and Tucker were singing a duet, and when they had finished, Conductor Fritz Stiedry turned toward the tenor and said: "Bravo Mr. Tucker." Tucker thereupon reached out an arm toward the baritone, and asked: "What about Guarrera?"

One anecdote from his early Met days gives an indication of his good nature. He had a fan in Philadelphia who always came backstage to see him after performances. For years, the fan would accompany Tucker out the door and hail a cab for him and Sara, who invariably accompanied her husband—and still does—on the road. After a certain *Rigoletto*—on a cold, rainy night—the fan insisted that they let him take them to a wonderful Jewish restaurant where the chef would fall all over himself cooking up any dish Tucker wanted. Tucker agreed and the trio got in a taxi. They started talking and soon the taxi driver got into the conversation. When they got to the restaurant, Tucker, wife, and fan went ahead. The taxi driver prepared to drive off, but Tucker turned around and said, "Where are *you* running to—come on in." He did. Then Tucker told the fan to call up his wife, and she came over and they had a party.

Moments like that, of course, helped relieve the grind of being on the road. "Look, there is opera, both here and on tour. There is recording. There is concert traveling. You sing and sing and sing. It's a miracle that the voice can stand up to it. Yet just singing, even a great deal of singing, won't hurt a voice. It's the rest of it. It's very hard to keep a family in this business. I know when I first started at the Met, great singers used to say to me, 'You're lucky to have that family.' 'Why?' I'd ask, 'when you have greatness?' But I got to understand because I saw them going home to their hotel rooms, alone. What did they have really? Nothing."

His managers would tell him in the 1950s, "Dick, you'll

never be an international opera star until you sing in
Europe, sing at La Scala." He would tell them he would
someday when he could go for at least two months.
"This going and singing for two weeks is no good, the
tension is wrong, the direction is strange," he said. "You
know, no singer is any good in a role until he has sung it at
least twenty-five times. Yes, I've sung *Forza* and *Don Carlo*,
but in a season, in a house I was used to. And then I don't
want to leave my family. My boys are growing up and I
want to be here to watch them grow. And then there's the
head of the house, you knew, in an Orthodox home. It is
important to me that I be here to oversee the education of
my sons. Of course, my oldest boy now is in college, but the
two little ones are still at home. And another thing: I like
America. I like to be able to go into the corner drugstore
and say 'Give me a Coke,' and you can't do that in Europe."

When Tucker did go abroad, it was to sing with the
likes of Renata Tebaldi and Maria Callas. To his great
regret, Tucker never recorded with Tebaldi, but some of
Callas's finest EMI recordings of the 1950s—notably *Forza*
and *Aïda*—were made with Tucker as her tenor. As much
as these things can be judged by an outsider, Tucker appears never to have had much trouble with them or any
other of his leading ladies—Albanese, Steber, Nilsson,
Caballé, Maliponte. Once during a rehearsal of *Andrea
Chénier* with Tebaldi, Tucker stopped the rehearsal during
the love duet. "She was too far away from me. When I sing
a love duet I've got to be near the woman I'm making love
to, or have her in my arms." He went to Tebaldi's dressing
room later to explain. "Her mother understood what I was
talking about, and she kissed me." As Tucker puts it with an
engagingly straight face: "All the leading ladies have always
liked me, and for one very good reason, they're singing

with a sincere artist. Our relationships have always been admirable, of the highest quality."

So, it seems, with Callas. When in the winter of 1965 she was returning to the Met for the two *Toscas* that would, as everybody guessed, turn out to be her swan song at the Met, she asked, so he says, for Tucker for both performances. They had performed together as far back as 1947, when she made her debut with him in Verona. "She had sprained her ankle and I held her up for two acts. That was something, because she weighed over two hundred pounds in those days.

At any rate, at the Met in 1965, Tucker could do only one *Tosca* (Corelli did the other). She did not want to rehearse. "She called me up and said, 'Richard, you know *Tosca*, I know *Tosca*, Fausto [Cleva] knows *Tosca*, why do we need to rehearse?" Tucker didn't see her until a few seconds before he went onstage. At the second intermission, she approached him and said, "Richard, why is it I always feel so comfortable working with you?" Tucker, still with an absolutely straight face, replied: "Maria, tonight you're in the major leagues."

As for male colleagues, tenors tend not to pal around with other tenors, but they do not mind baritones at all. One of Tucker's earliest chums was Frank Guarrera, that master of the Italian comic touch, who used to refer to himself and Tucker as "the gold dust twins." Much later, in the 1970s, Tucker would hook up with Robert Merrill for a continuing series of joint coast-to-coast recitals. In the 1950s, though, Tucker worked most with the great, but at the time unaccountably underrated, Verdi baritone Leonard Warren in countless *Boccanegras*, *Rigolettos*, *Toscas*, and *Forzas*.

One evening in March 1960, during a performance of *Forza*, Warren finished Don Carlo's aria "Urna fatale del mio destin" (Fatal urn of my destiny) turned to his left preparing to make his exit, then collapsed in the middle of the stage. From the wings, Tucker ran out crying, "Lennie, Lennie, what is it?" At forty-eight, Warren was dead of a cerebral hemorrhage. The performance did not resume. Said a faint-voiced Tucker the next morning: "He didn't show any signs of illness, he didn't show anything at all. I was standing backstage on the 39th Street side joking with Bing and Agathe [Warren's wife], and I motioned her to come closer to the wings to hear him sing. I was joking around— they call me the joker at the Met. The minute he stopped singing I looked and saw that he had fallen on his face. I thought he had tripped but there was nothing he could have fallen on and I knew something was wrong. I yelled 'Pull down the curtain!' and ran over to him. I was the first to reach him. It reminded me of the scene with Paul Muni in *The Last Angry Man* when he tries to rouse the dead man.

"I kept saying to him 'Lennie, get back to yourself.' Then the doctor was there and started rubbing his heart. He said immediately it was a stroke, not a heart attack as there was no pulse. Then the other doctor came too. It was horrible. I will never forget it. Lennie worked like a dog on *Simon Boccanegra*. I know as I've been living with him the last thirty days. Every single day we worked on it and we were doing other performances as well, and it just took its toll of him." Tucker then went on: "This is the tragic folly of life—he is honored in death but not in life. This was the greatest, most underrated baritone of our time. I am very happy to have been associated with him for fifteen years."


In his later years at the Met, Tucker began to assume the role of elder statesman, offering advice when asked, throwing out some old jokes backstage to help lighten the tension. "The young singers call me big brother," he says, "and the door is always open and I tell them the right thing to do." Essentially, he wants to be approached, wants to be helpful, wants, to a certain extent, to be idolized. That is why he may be the only major singer at the Met to have both his phone numbers—in Great Neck and Manhattan—listed in the telephone directory, as opposed to the usual fetish for unlisted numbers. He wants that one fan, or chance acquaintance, to be able to get through to him. "Who knows? It may be some poor guy who just wants to come backstage that night with his wife and kids. I say, let him come. It can be a festive occasion for him." Or: "People think I'm a father confessor. I can't destroy that."

As to his ability to impart his wisdom or knowledge of technique, he does not seem to have the gift. His basic belief is that singing is singing, and technique, technique. The suggestion, proffered by so many singing teachers, that one instructional technique may work for one singer, but not another, is something that drives him to fury. "I have never been invited in twenty-eight years to sing before the singing teachers' association. Why? Because twenty-five years ago I called them a bunch of butchers. What's bad for one is good for another? I don't believe it." When asked how a singer communicates, he wanders through a generality, and then returns to his own experiences—where, by and large, he is on safe ground. "Communication through singing is a combination of voice and conveying the meaning of the words. Some people say I give too much when I sing. I don't know how to sing any other way. That's why I have so many fans. They see I'm pouring my heart out. When I'm singing about jealousy, how can I be calm?" When asked what goes through his mind when he is onstage, it turns out that he is thinking primarily about a commodity that has to be delivered. "I see people, and when I go out onstage I always get the feeling these people have paid to get the best. They want no apologies. If the artist can't give his best, he shouldn't appear. There should be no announcements—as there have been at the Met recently—that this artist or that will sing under duress. That helps create a gulf between the company and the public. And that's why I always strive to give a better performance this time than last time."

It was in October 1973 that Tucker realized one of his most cherished dreams—to sing the role of Eléazar in Halévy's *La Juive* (*The Jewess*) in full staging. There were two things about the role that always intrigued Tucker. One was that it was a part associated with Martinelli and Gigli, but especially with Caruso. It was the last thing Caruso ever sang, and to many it was his greatest role. The second was that Eléazar is an elderly Jewish patriarch who performs an entire Passover Seder service within the opera. Over the years, there was talk of reviving *La Juive* for Tucker at the Met, but nothing ever materialized, and currently, with the Met holding tight reins on its new-production dollars, it seems unlikely that he will ever do it there. There was even talk of a production for Tucker in Chicago in 1957, but that, too, fell through. All Tucker could manage previously were two concert performances—the first in New York with the Friends of French Opera in 1964, the second in London during the winter of 1973. The latter performance, luckily enough, led to an RCA LP of excerpts of *La Juive* that was released in the spring of 1974 and strenuously whetted the appetite for the entire work starring Tucker.

When the night finally came for Tucker's first staged performance, it was at the New Orleans Opera. That was just fine with him, since *La Juive* was given its American

Richard Tucker as Eléazar in Halévy's *La Juive* (*Photo Courtesy RCA Records*)

premiere in New Orleans in 1844, and Tucker, as it happens, is a great champion of regional opera. "It's very important. Don't forget, the three or four big companies are not enough for a country with 200,000,000 people. There must be a need for regional opera, otherwise people would not support it." Once the performance was over, no one could fail to see why Tucker had been attracted to the work. Eléazar is a Jewish goldsmith who is driven to use his foster daughter as an instrument of revenge against his Christian oppressors. His aria "Rachel, quand du Seigneur" is one of the great things in the tenor literature. Most of the critics, who had descended on New Orleans from as far away as New York and San Francisco, came away convinced that Tucker's Eléazar was something that should be heard not only in their own hometowns, but everywhere that great operatic performances are cherished and properly displayed. For the performance, Tucker wore Caruso's old costume, which had been found in the Met's archives, and, wrote Charles L. DuFour in the New Orleans *States-Item:* "Last night the mantle of the great Caruso literally and figuratively fell upon [Tucker's] shoulders. . . . Tucker, both vocally and historically, projected effectively the conflicting emotions that surged within the breast of Eléazar—reverence and devotion to the faith of his fathers, tender love for his foster daughter Rachel, and implacable hatred of his enemies, with the spirit of revenge for the persecution of himself and his people."

Tucker was by now working at the Met for his fourth general manager, Schuyler Chapin. Chapin had succeeded Goeran Gentele, who was so tragically killed in an automobile accident in July 1972 only days after assuming the post. Gentele's predecessor was, of course, Bing, and on the night of April 22, 1972, it came time to say farewell to the man who had done so much for the company in general, and Tucker in particular. And what a farewell it was. All the stars—Caballé, Nilsson, Price, Żylis-Gara, Resnik, Domingo, Corelli, Milnes, to name but a few—came out on the Met stage in evening dress and serenaded Bing and a gala audience with arias until the early hours of the morning.

For Tucker, however, the evening spoke not so much of endings, but of at least one new beginning. One of the hits of the event was his duet with baritone Robert Merrill, "Invano, Alvaro" from Verdi's *La Forza del Destino*. That their voices blended majestically was only one way in which Tucker and the former Moishe Miller were two of a kind. Both were New Yorkers, both had gone to Manhattan's New Utrecht High, both had joined the Met in 1945 (Merrill as the elder Germont in *Traviata*), both were Americans in a house still dedicated to the proposition that all singers were entitled to an equal opportunity, unless they came from Europe, in which case they were more equal.

And so they began giving a series of joint recitals and appearances with symphony orchestras on tour throughout the United States. The audiences loved it, and the local critics would invariably use the occasion to trot out their rarely used glossary of superlatives. A one-night stand in Indianapolis in January 1974 with conductor Izler Solomon and the Indianapolis Symphony Orchestra, according to critic Corbin Patrick of the *Star*, "resulted in vocal fireworks that probably could be matched today only by recalling the likes of Caruso and Scotti from opera's legendary golden age." Tucker, said Patrick, "sang from the tips of his well-polished shoes," and "first cracked the audience's reserve wide open with his super-charged singing of the popular aria, 'Vesti la giubba' from Leoncavallo's *Pagliacci*." As for Merrill, his way was "charm and subtlety, with restraint

in keeping with the limitations conventionally imposed by
the concert stage." The Tucker-Merrill road show also
would find the two singers popping up at colleges or local
opera clubs, to engage in question-and-answer sessions.
Talking to the young music students interested Tucker
especially. "We give it to 'em straight from the shoulder.
No phony answers to their questions. We tell them, don't
make art a joke. Don't move too fast. People will recognize
you if you are serious. If you're not, don't waste your own
time or your parents' money."

And then home again to Great Neck. In the good old
days, the term *golden age* could almost as well have been
applied to the life-styles of the singers as to their music.
A tenor—especially a tenor—might sleep late, rise in time
for a starchy and stuffing Italian meal, washed down with
flagons of red wine. The meal would be at the artist's
favorite restaurant,, which would in time mount his picture in the front window, or even name itself after him.
In the afternoon, the artist would rehearse drowsily, or, if
he could get out of that, lurch back to his apartment and
slumber until performance time. After the opera, it would
be a late supper, more wine, more celebration, more (in
most cases) women, and then to bed in the wee hours.

Richard Tucker rises each day at 8 A.M. for a breakfast
of Special K, orange juice, skimmed milk, and coffee. And
then, if he does not go off to the Met or to his "office"
apartment in Manhattan, he proceeds to live the life of a
suburban John Doe. "You know, in Europe tenors are gods,
but they have to live up to the legend, too. In America,
people take everything for granted. So you're the greatest
tenor in the world, so what?" For years, while the boys were
young, Tucker would be there for the Little League sessions, or, if the family had gotten home late, he would

drive them around on their newspaper routes. "Sometimes I felt like the milkman." From all outward appearances, Tucker is in astonishingly good health. His face remains almost babyish in its smoothness, and though twenty or so pounds overweight, he carries it well and is obviously comfortable. He is a natty dresser who looks good in a turtleneck, tweedy sportswear, or padded double-breasted suit. As often as he can, in New York or, say, Miami Beach —a favorite watering hole during the winter—he adjourns to a health club where "I take my massages and whirlpools." He is essentially a nonreader, but enjoys social dancing. "People ask me how it is I'm such a good dancer, and I say, 'Look, what do you expect, I paid my $69 at the Concord Hotel.' Yes sir, I learned my cha-cha-chas and my tangos." Dancing, sports, dining out, movies, television, parties—"You name it," says Tucker, "I like to do it. I'm the all-American boy."

How long will the all-American boy continue to present himself to the world as Richard Tucker? "As long as I have my good health and can deliver to the people. When I cannot give to the audience the best of Richard Tucker, that's when I'll retire."

# Jon Vickers

BY

*John Ardoin*

J ON VICKERS is a study in contradictions, a very private person in a very public profession. Like all great singers, the Canadian tenor has earned admiration, but he has also been the object of outright hostility. While few are willing to detract from his voice, he has been accused of being arrogant, aloof, and extremely difficult to work with.

Much of this criticism has grown out of the enormous contrasts to be found within the man himself. Vickers shuns parties, interviews, and nonprofessional contact with his colleagues. And yet, while he has steadfastly refused to engage a publicist, answer his critics, or indulge himself in any of the self-serving ego trips typical of most performers, he frequently displays a pressing need to be accepted and appreciated.

Vickers can be an extrovert, slapping people on the back

or sweeping them up and swinging them in the air; or an introvert, returning a greeting with a blank look, or with measured distance in his voice and manner. While he is fervently sought by all the major opera houses and has inspired a staunch following among those who believe that opera is first a forum for expression, he has rarely made inroads with the fan element which hangs around the stage door, forms claques, and attempts to delve into the private lives of singers and call them by their first names.

Vickers's approach to life appears simple at first, even puritanical, but it masks a complexity which, although baffling, has aided him in understanding and portraying a wide range of human behavior. In short, the man is as arresting as the artist—an uncommon occurrence among singers.

At the age of thirty, Vickers was catapulted into prominence in 1957 when the Royal Opera in London mounted a landmark production of Berlioz's epic *Les Troyens*. Sixteen years later, *Les Troyens* at last reached the Metropolitan Opera. The first New York staging of the work was the most heralded event of the 1973–74 season, and the Aeneas was again Vickers.

In a very real sense, Vickers's career came full circle with *Troyens*, for the opera launched his international career, and he repeated it in New York at the very height of his fame as the leading dramatic tenor of the day. In the decades between the two *Troyens* productions, Vickers's operatic ascendancy has been steady and brilliant. He sang at the Vienna Opera, La Scala, the Bayreuth and Salzburg Festivals, and with the companies of San Francisco, Chicago, and Dallas as Radames, Otello, Canio, Andrea Chénier, Don José, Siegmund, Parsifal, Tristan, Giason, Florestan, Samson, and Peter Grimes. He has recorded seven of

Jon Vickers as Aeneas in Berlioz's *Les Troyens* (*Photo by Erika Davidson*)

these roles as well as Aeneas for major record labels and has filmed *Otello, Carmen,* and *Pagliacci.*

A dramatic tenor traditionally makes ringing sounds of great power but little subtlety. The norm for a Tristan or Otello has become endurance and heroics, and a dramatic tenor tends to be a limited stylist. Vickers endures and is an authentic hero whose voice is geared to mighty statements, but he also sings his gallery of roles with an extraordinary range of sensitivity, style, and immaculate pitch, plus the line and mezza voce of a lyric tenor and an agility which puts him as much at home with Handel as with Wagner.

"Great dramatic singing," observed English critic David Cairns, "is, almost by definition, singing that is disliked by as many people as passionately admire it; the quality that strikes one man to the soul grates on another man's nerves. I can well imagine Vickers not being a favourite singer of that type of operagoer who treats singing as a higher form of interior decoration and opera as the glorification of bel canto. But without doubt there are others too, confirmed believers in the gospel of opera as drama, who simply do not take to the individual timbre and manner through which he expresses the outsize emotions that are his natural element."

Vickers has been accused of "crooning," of exaggerating his mezza voce, of allowing "emotion to obliterate singing," and of failing to blend his registers. But there are also those who speak of Maria Callas—a singer Vickers venerates— only in terms of her wobble or harshness of sound. To limit either Vickers or Callas to their "faults" is to miss the point entirely. If either sang differently or more "correctly," they would not be themselves. Their "faults" are like fingerprints—sounds and a manner of performance which make them at once identifiable and unlike any other. It is a price paid willingly or unwillingly by their public for something unique. The fact that Vickers again and again recalls Callas through his individual mode of singing explains to a degree some of the heated words he has inspired the length and breadth of the music world.

Vickers simply doesn't do what is expected of him by tradition as a dramatic tenor. He is not an exhibitionist. Restraint is a major part of his makeup and art—an interior reserve of force. As Cairns puts it, "He is the least ranting and posturing of tenors, the most formidable in dignity and inner strength. You feel that what comes out is only a fraction of what stirs and seethes within. This sense of turbulent energy held under stubborn control can generate a tension unequalled in opera today. When Vickers plays an introverted character goaded to violence—Canio, Don José, Otello—the whole house sits as though on the edge of a volcano. In the final scene of *Pagliacci* . . . his explosions of fury were the more terrible for the stillness that preceded them; sheer intensity of suffering forced a breach in the grim façade, through which you glimpsed a hell of jealousy. The anguish of Vickers's Canio lifted the work temporarily onto the plane of tragedy. . . . Vickers belongs to that élite of opera-singers whose grandeur and veracity of utterance justify the pretensions of the genre. That is what it is all about, and for this one waits and keeps the flame of one's faith alight."

The contradictions in Vickers are in large measure part of a wall he has raised for self-protection, as though he regarded much of the outer world as alien and not to be trusted. This wall has arisen from the philosophy Jonathan Stewart Vickers has developed as an artist and from a life-style which is the product of a strict, religious upbringing

in the small Canadian community of Prince Albert in Sas-
katchewan, where his father was principal of the local
school and the town's bandmaster.

"My father was away at band practice when I was born,"
Vickers recalls. "My mother was alone; it was a very cold
wintry night late in October 1926. There was no running
water or electricity in the old house, only a well in the
backyard. We moved from there shortly after I reached my
fourth birthday. Later we had to move again, for the
Depression was really terrible at that time—about 1932—
and on a schoolmaster's salary with eight children the
second house became too great a responsibility; we had to
find cheaper accommodations. I remember during this time
that my father went off to work for a friend, not so much
to earn extra money as to ensure one less mouth at home
to feed.

"Traditionally, children are supposed to hate school. I
don't know whether it was an act or not, but I never did.
I can still smell my school in my nostrils. To me, it was
nothing but fun—the study, the schoolroom, and most of
all the playground with its swings, baseball, and football.
I remember, too, the city used to flood the playground in
winter, and we kids couldn't wait to get out in the afternoon to skate until suppertime. I loved romping in the
snow and sliding down what I thought then were mon-
strously big hills. We had big leather patches on our
seats and knees and used to slide on these down the ice
slopes."

Yet, it was not school which ultimately proved the
greatest influence on Vickers during his formative years.
His most compelling memories are of the summers when
school was out spent working on a farm. "From the age of
eight to eighteen, I came back to the farm each year. I

have a lot of wonderful memories of it—biscuits and milk
before going to bed at night, getting up early in the morning, ice in the rain barrel, huge country breakfasts with a
happy crowd of workmen, teams of horses to be harnessed
and barns to be cleaned out, out in the field at daybreak
pitching sheaves, and the haying season itself. I used to love
the rich hay, even though I was mocked because I didn't
know how to use a pitchfork. They never trusted me with
the stacking either; I was a city fella.

"As I look back at it now, I realize my whole philosophy
of life was formed in these years. In this rural setting I
came to the conclusion the only meaningful thing in this
life is contact with other human beings. It was there, too,
that deep and profound Christian convictions settled in
me which have been an influence all of my life. The understanding, which slowly and surely developed in me, of the
necessity of human contact and an understanding of the
needs of others and their problems, has probably, more
than anything else, given me the ability to analyze my
roles, to come to grips with a score, to study a drama, to
project my feelings into the life of someone I've never met
except on a piece of paper. It enabled me to put myself
into that person's life and their feelings to the point that I
can put the person on and wear him for my stage life.

"It is a strange sensation, after what I've done in the
world and in my career, to go back to the farm where it all
began. The nostalgia I feel makes much of what has followed seem sort of pointless and silly, for the real lessons
of life are back there in the earth, in the relationships I
formed, and in the friendships which have supported me
through my whole life.

"To this day, I still have a perhaps unrealistic yearning
to be a farmer. Of course, one marvelous by-product of a

successful career is being able to afford my own farm. A lot of people must think I'm only a gentleman farmer, but I am deeply involved in the operation of my farm. And I often say to my wife Henrietta, and sometimes to my colleagues, that when I get fed up with the dirty dirt of my profession, I go home and work amongst the clean dirt of my avocation. People, however, don't always understand when I talk of the effect soil has on me and of my love of the earth. They think of it only in abstract terms, I guess. But when you sit on a tractor for hours and watch the sod turn and be buried in the dirt, you develop a great affection for that thing people call dirt and I call soil. Soil brings a sense of accomplishment—growing beautiful crops, producing one's own food, making flower beds, watching the cycle of life. This rejuvenates me, recharges me.

"I find it tremendously satisfying to throw around bales of hay, sit on a tractor, drive a baler. And while I do these things, I do a tremendous amount of reflecting on values. In such moments, I find myself saying, 'What am I doing in this crazy opera business?' It is one of the sad aspects of my job that art is a profession, and while art is divine, the profession is terrible. This builds strong resentments in me, for so many times I have had to battle against foreign elements which have crept into the arts, people who turn art inside out and misuse it for their own glorification."

To Vickers, a singer is not a narcissistic entity, but a servant to art, the composer, and music. He has had few colleagues who were his peer in this regard. One was Callas. "There are those who claim to follow in the footsteps of Callas, and this is really amusing to me. Maria took these old, old operas written for specific voices in that terrible era when singers were abysmally conceited and dictated with whom they would sing and what they would sing.

They misused music to demonstrate only vocal virtuosity. Now, Maria had as much virtuosity as any singer ever had, but she made it serve a greater end. She served the composer and made music a real dramatic experience. Through her fiery determination, she demonstrated that every moment onstage had to be a living thing. Mind you, I have a great admiration today for Joan Sutherland and Beverly Sills, but, alas, I despair that they are holding back the onward movement of opera as a dramatic art, using opera to demonstrate their particular vocal techniques instead of serving what I consider to be the greater absolute, the drama itself, the meaning of the words."

These principles forcefully return to Vickers when he returns to the farm and the soil. "It might seem strange to talk about the most profound aspects of one's thinking as far as art is concerned while sitting in a big, empty barn, swept out and ready for a new crop of wheat. But the very fact of being back to 'simplistics' and to the elements of life turns my thinking to what is happening in my profession and the necessity of purifying the art form. It makes me very sad that so many in the arts do not give this question much thought. I'm only connected with one very small aspect of art, but I feel in the whole history of civilization, it is the arts that have led men toward truth. Those who touch the arts—whether through painting, the stage, music, dance, or sculpture—must return to the original idealism that started them on their career and serve truth in art. And we need idealism not only in art but in life. Maybe I will sound old-fashioned, but I think a fundamental dishonesty has crept into our way of life today. With the fantastic power of modern communications and the unbelievable shrinking of the world, we have been given the opportunity to capitalize on the ignorant, to view them only as markets, to corrupt them for our own purposes, to thrust twisted ideas of life down their throats which in our heart of hearts we know are not true, not honest, but which is done for no other reason than a worshiping of the almighty dollar."

Vickers's philosophy of life and art stems directly from his upbringing. He came from a large family, and his father, a staunch Lutheran-Presbyterian, was strict with the family, though his mother—from the same background—was a bit more liberal. "Our upbringing ruled out moving pictures and dancing, and we weren't allowed to ride our bicycles on Sunday. The piano in our home, which was always in use, was never played on Sunday except for hymns. It was an atmosphere not all in the family responded to. In fact, a couple rebelled against it. As for myself, I enjoyed it. I think it probably gave me my tremendous incentive for accomplishment.

"My father believed one should not necessarily strive for excellence in any particular field, but should accept the situation in which one found oneself, and within that framework, do one's utmost. He constantly quoted a verse of scripture that says 'Do with one's might what one's hand finds to do.' I found security in that discipline, and I do feel it made an indelible imprint on my whole personality. I think it made me uncompromising in my demands on myself, made me feel that whenever I had failed in what I had asked of myself, I'd let God down, I'd let myself down, I'd let my profession down, I'd let my talent down.

"As a product of upbringing, and because I was given a talent, I feel it is wickedness if people do not use their gifts to the ultimate of their effort and serve the ultimate in art. I am impatient, I am sure—no, I am certain—with my colleagues if I find one using my art form for his own glorification. I don't believe that is the right order of things. A person's talent must serve art; art must not be made to serve the person."

This lofty attitude toward art is one thing which has set Vickers apart in the world of opera and has created some of his difficulties in his relationships with others. Schuyler Chapin, general manager of the Metropolitan Opera, was once asked if Vickers was a difficult man to work with. "Absolutely," he replied, "but for the right reasons. He is not difficult in the sense of personal vanity; he is difficult in the sense that he demands perfection of himself and therefore demands it of others. You can't fault someone for that."

Vickers insists, "I could never think of myself as an entertainer. I sincerely believe the stage is a moral institution, and it should always have a tremendous social message to make people examine themselves and their attitudes towards all things in life. Of course, there is some opera that is pure entertainment. A real good performance of *Così fan tutte* is sheer entertainment, although beneath it there is something that digs at you. There are barbs in *Così*, as there are in all of Mozart's operas."

In effect, Vickers is echoing the view of conductor Colin Davis, with whom he recorded *Les Troyens:* "Operas that are merely decorative don't interest Jon very much, and they don't interest me either. I think we share a rather severe attitude toward our work." But to whatever use Vickers puts his voice, a love of singing has been as deep and necessary a part of him as his love of the earth.

"My first recollections of singing in public was when I was about five years old. I was in the church choir, sang solos, and entertained the prisoners in the local jail during services conducted by my father. I remember my sisters were whistled at by the prisoners and I sang 'Don't Forget the Promise Made to Mother.' All those hard criminals shed tears listening to that curly-headed little fella—not much hair left there now—singing about the promises made on Mother's Day.

"I grew up in a very musical atmosphere. All my family played instruments and sang. I was always performing duets, trios, and quartets with my brothers and sisters. My two older brothers were in the city band and took music lessons. I never did. I guess everyone thought of singing as a natural talent; you just opened your mouth and sang. Most people still think that's all there is to singing. Anyway, then I sang for anybody, anywhere, anytime because it was fun. I didn't care if my voice cracked; I didn't care if I sang well or not. Fundamentally, I now realize I was doing it to satisfy something I needed in myself."

A farmer for whom Vickers worked as a boy also remembers his great need to sing. "The young people were very fond of meetings and they'd always ask Jonny to sing. He never hesitated, though I recall one time they accused him of showing off a bit, and so he said he wouldn't sing. But I went to him and asked, 'Who gave you your voice anyway, Jonny?' 'Well, God did,' he answered. 'Then,' I said, 'Sing, sing sing!' And he sang and kept on singing."

When Vickers returns to Canada now and to his old friends, they don't understand why he no longer joins in their singsongs, why he doesn't sing for the fun of it in their living rooms. "One thing they don't realize now that I'm a professional, is that if I sang in their house, they would wonder what had happened. It would sound like a truck or a cannon. When you've been trained to sing from a stage over a 100-piece orchestra and in auditoriums which seat thousands, it's a different kind of sound than you make in a living room.

"Now, when they ask me to sing, I make up all kinds of jokes, like saying 'I don't sing unless I get paid for it.' I suppose that's fundamentally true, but when you are in the profession, you cannot sing unless you do it with absolute seriousness. It's your job; you have trained yourself to seek a standard. It is a wrench to your whole system, your whole way of thinking, your whole way of feeling to sing unless you have prepared yourself emotionally, vocally, and physically to open your mouth. This is something a layman just can't understand; it's caused a lot of misunderstanding for me."

Despite the part singing played in Vickers's early life, he did not initially consider it as a profession. His first ambition was to be a farmer and then a doctor. But a potential career in medicine was cut short when returning war veterans were given priority in Canada's schools, and Vickers could not gain entrance. He went to work first as a branch manager for Standard Brands, then worked for Woolworth's, and finally settled in Winnipeg as an agent for the Hudson's Bay Company. During this time, he appeared in amateur and semiprofessional musicals, singing everything from Gilbert and Sullivan to *Naughty Marietta*. It was during performances of the Victor Herbert operetta in Winnipeg in 1949 that Vickers met soprano Mary Morrison, who was so impressed with his voice that she urged him to try for a scholarship at Toronto's Royal Conservatory of Music.

To his surprise, he was accepted and began study with his only voice teacher, George Lambert. "I remember when I first met Lambert, I told him, 'The moment you think I have reached a limit, let me know. I have no intention of beating my head against the wall if there are limitations to my voice. Tell me at once, and I'll pack it in.' " But Lambert found no need for his young tenor "to pack it in"; he was more than pleased with Vickers's progress. During this period Vickers prepared and sang some fifteen roles for the Canadian Broadcasting Corporation, as well as a wide range of oratorio from the Bach masses and passions to Handel's *Judas Maccabaeus* and *Samson* and Haydn's *Creation*.

He also made his first recording, a *Messiah* conducted by the late Sir Ernest MacMillan, and was a member of the Canadian Opera Company in Toronto, appearing in such unlikely roles as the Duke in *Rigoletto*, Ferrando in *Così*, and Alfred in *Die Fledermaus*. Yet, Vickers still had misgivings about making a career as a singer. But another singer had no doubts. After the first rehearsal for a production of *Carmen* by the Canadian Opera featuring mezzo-soprano Regina Resnik, she asked her José, Vickers, "Where have you been hiding?" 'Oh,' he said, 'I'm just a Canadian tenor and don't know if I'll continue or go back to the farm.' 'No,' I told him, 'Maybe one day you'll own a farm, but you're not going *back* to the farm.'"

During the *Carmen* period, Miss Resnik was asked about the feasibility of performing Britten's *The Rape of Lucretia* for the next Stratford Festival. She had taken part in the American premiere of the work as a soprano and recounts, "I had sung the Female Chorus, knew the work well, and knew what a problem it could be casting the Male Chorus. So when they asked me about the work, I said 'You haven't any problem, because you already have a great tenor for the Male Chorus. He's singing Don José now.'"

Thanks to Resnik's recommendation, Vickers went to Stratford for *The Rape*. It was now a case of "How are you going to keep him down on the farm after he's sung Don José?" Following Stratford, Vickers was asked to audition for Covent Garden. The late Sir David Webster, then director of the company, was encouraging but no contract materialized. A year later, Vickers still had had no word from the Garden and again became discouraged. The last engagement scheduled for him at that time was in June 1956. He resolved to give up singing professionally if nothing significant happened to his career by that date. A month before his self-imposed deadline, a telegram arrived from Sir David offering Vickers a three-year contract. On April 27, 1957, he made his debut at the Royal Opera as Riccardo in *Un Ballo in Maschera*, and less than two months later sang his first *Troyens*. The rest, as cliché has it, is history.

If Vickers were pressed to choose a favorite part, no doubt it would be Britten's Peter Grimes, for he favors roles that are complex not only in their vocal challenges but in their dramatic and intellectual demands as well. Also Grimes is the role in which the man and the singer, together with their contradictions, are most closely united. "He is Peter Grimes," says Colin Davis, who conducted the memorable new production of the work for Vickers at the Metropolitan Opera in 1967. "He has that touch of inspired madness the character demands, together with an incredible physical presence and a strength which fits a fisherman. He also has a kind of radiance, a childlike innocence; there is something incredibly sympathetic about him. He draws on all of these qualities in *Grimes*, and it is probably his greatest creation."

To Vickers, "*Grimes* is, of all the operas I sing, the absolute prototype of what I think opera should be. I do not consider Grimes as an individual. Intentionally my costuming is very simple, my makeup very extreme, my gamut of emotions very wide, because though *Grimes* is the story of

Jon Vickers in the title role of Britten's *Peter Grimes* (*Photo by Louis Mélançon*)

a fisherman, he is the timeless symbol of all rejection by society. Britten has used Grimes to demonstrate the enormous human problem of lack of identity. It is very pertinent to our times and universal in its message. Grimes is an outcast because he is misunderstood. He is a crotchety person, difficult to deal with. In rejecting him, society has put Grimes under such pressure that the poor man finally goes mad. The breaking point comes when the girl he loves, Ellen, joins the others in turning against him. He tries to prove he can make himself acceptable by earning a lot of money. This, too, is pertinent to today."

The Met's *Grimes* was staged by Sir Tyrone Guthrie. If he did not know it prior to the production, he quickly learned that Vickers takes an active part in the staging of an opera in which he appears. Here is a tenor who might well be a graduate of Actors Studio, so concerned is he in having motivations, of understanding the necessity of a gesture or a movement. Sometimes his intensity carries him too far. "I'll never forget," says Davis, "in the middle of a fraught rehearsal with the chorus, Guthrie shouting at Jon, 'Vickers, for Chrissake, go sit down and shut up.' And Jon, like a lamb, went and sat down and shut up. I've never loved him more."

The production of *Grimes* was revived in 1973, and Vickers changed a number of points on which he had disagreed with Guthrie. "I thought he had me treat Grimes's young apprentice too harshly in the original," he admits. "I wouldn't handle my own son that way, although I'd be rough and tough with him when necessary. There have been times when I have come home in a bad mood because of something that had nothing to do with my son, and I've seen a frightened child; he could feel my anger. I applied this in *Grimes.* When Grimes returns to his hut in a flaming temper, it is because he is angry that Ellen has deserted him and because he had let his temper rule him and had slapped her. Grimes, however, is not angry with the boy, but the boy is terrified because of Grimes's temper. When the lad starts to sob, he gets through to Grimes, and in that moment, I try in a clumsy way to comfort him. This is all mine, not Sir Tyrone's."

Bringing his own emotions and experiences to his roles is of a vital concern to Vickers, and he is able to make such applications even in situations which are foreign to his own feelings, as in *Otello*. "I've been close to *Otello* since I was a student. I originally learned the role in 1952 when I was asked to sing it for CBC. I refused the offer at first, then they asked me if I would cover the part and do some of the rehearsals to spare them added expense. This I agreed to; they paid me $100 as the official understudy. In the days when you are a student, you are so worried—or at least, I was—that I learned the opera in its entirety, everyone's part. I have loved *Otello* ever since. In 1960, I was asked to sing it with Tullio Serafin for my first opera recording. I really didn't think I could keep turning down offers for the part, especially when given the chance to work with a master conductor like Serafin. But after recording it, I decided I shouldn't sing it onstage for another year or two. Finally, I performed it for the first time in Buenos Aires and have sung it a lot since then, although I do put a limit on the number of *Otello*s I will sing a year—no more than eight.

"At the moment there are really only two of us—Jimmy McCracken and myself—who sing Otello in the first houses. If I let myself, I'd be singing only *Otello*s all the time, and no voice can take that. However, one of the wonderful things about a part like Otello is the breadth of scope and the interpretative possibilities it offers. Each of them is valid; that's the greatness of the work. There are many people—and they drive me crazy and I have no patience with them—who decide that such and such an artist has the definitive interpretation of a role. I call that utter nonsense. None of us who have performed Otello, and I include Martinelli, the great Ramon Vinay, Del Monaco, and McCracken, are capable of taking this work and showing it to the public in all its profundity and magnificence. We all have our limitations and we all have our insecurities as far as this part is concerned. Otello is of such incredible difficulties and of such genius and greatness, no one singer in a three-hour performance could encompass it completely.

"I have the greatest respect and admiration for what others have done with the role, and I think anyone who sings it must bring to Otello his own experiences, knowledge, sensitivities, fears, jealousies, and hatred. However, you must remember that the way Jimmy McCracken manifests jealousy, for example, is vastly different from the way I do. Jealousy from my standpoint as a man would not be easily discernible. It would be an inward thing. My approach to Otello is as a great human being who suffers inside. He is a smoldering, boiling caldron. When he bursts out, he really bursts out, but he immediately clamps the lid on himself again. This tremendous inner tension and the menacing quality of Otello must be present even when he seems very calm and in control. This is my approach because it is how I would behave in a similar situation. Others explode when they are jealous, when they are hurt. I do not. Mine is inner suffering, inner reactions, inner rage."

In performing *Otello* or *Carmen,* for example, Vickers

feels it is essential to have the best colleagues possible about him to achieve his characterization. "There are singers who want weak singers in other roles because they feel they come off better. I'm not of that school. Give me the strongest possible Iago, for the stronger is Iago the stronger is Otello. If you get a hammy, vulgar Iago, Otello comes out a jackass. Don José is much the same. Sometimes I have gotten myself into trouble with my leading ladies because I feel Carmen's life is best told through the eyes of Don José, through his breakdown. This in turn reflects the personality and quality of Carmen to the audience. If José is really caught up in her, tied in knots, then every man in the audience will be as well. To know Carmen best, one must see her through the devotion, passion, youth, idealism, and desires of José."

Part of the integral interpretation of a role for Vickers is applying his own makeup. It is a facet of performance he feels is vital and personal, though he tends to apologize for having to use pancake, liner, and eye shadow, as though this somehow reflects on his manliness. "My performance begins the moment I sit down in front of my makeup table. As I begin to apply Otello's coloring, for example, I also start to put on his personality as well. I must be a part of the physical change which takes place in order for the necessary mental change to take place as well. Yet, sometimes as I'm putting the muck on my face, I think, 'What a perfectly ridiculous way to make a living.' But I suppose everyone has unpleasant aspects to their jobs; makeup is one of mine.

"However, I feel this way only at the outset, because gradually the makeup process involves me and becomes quite absorbing. Naturally, more goes into a characterization than makeup. For instance, in my case I cannot

Jon Vickers in the title role of Verdi's *Otello* (*Photo by Erika Davidson*)

separate the way I interpret a role from my fundamental belief that in every human being there is a capacity for good and a capacity for evil. These are in different proportions from person to person and what makes people individual is the way in which such basic facets are balanced —one person's jealousy against another's lack of jealousy; one's maliciousness against another's warm, outgoing kindness.

"When I begin to analyze a role, first I decide what the dramatic balance is within the character. Then, I seek to find the same characteristics within myself and discover what I must exaggerate, consciously distort in me to make Otello, for example, real. I do this cold-bloodedly. It is a mental thing, not a matter of emotion. Once this is set, it never varies. I don't think my approach to Otello today is essentially different from when I initially studied the part. At that time, I reread all of Shakespeare, not just *Othello*, but all the plays. I went away on my holiday that year with five commentaries on *Othello* and read them all. So, I formed a very strong picture of what this man is. I think I have probably developed in my ability to demonstrate the character and his feelings, but I don't think my conception has changed. On the other hand, I don't think anyone can escape the natural evolution that takes place in a person's life and a singer's voice. At thirty-one you cannot project the calm of a man of forty-six. Otello sits more naturally within me now, because there are many aspects of character I no longer have to create artificially as I did in the beginning."

Vickers is none too happy with his recording of *Otello* made with Serafin and is relieved a new version with Herbert von Karajan will soon be issued. "The first recording of *Otello* is a travesty. It is not representative of my work at the time, and it is certainly not representative of my work today. If I have made one major mistake in my career, it was the signing of a contract with RCA. It was a contract, I might add, that I broke, and they did not have the nerve to bring proceedings against me. *Otello* was made in Rome with a terrible orchestra, and the recording schedule was impossibly arranged. The first day I recorded Otello's death five times. The second day I had to record the entrance of Otello in act one four times. Then, Tito Gobbi and I recorded the big duet 'Sì, pel ciel' seven times one day, twice the next. The quartet was recorded fourteen times, and I counted up to seventeen takes for the third-act finale and then stopped counting. A human voice cannot stand that kind of punishment, and all of it was for an orchestra to play the right notes.

"In the end, RCA made a recording in which the orchestra plays no wrong notes, but one with a very, very tired soprano, tenor, and baritone. I am not terribly happy with the *Aïda* for RCA [now available on London] either, even though it won an award. Here we were coping with a very domineering conductor in the person of Georg Solti, and his prime concern was not us but the sound of his orchestra. In fact, he actually told us in a number of places not to bother singing because he intended to drown us out anyway. Nor do I think Leontyne Price was presented at her best, and that is not at all condemning Leontyne. I think it is shocking when a recording company for the sake of a dollar would force a great singer like Leontyne to repeat and repeat a section until her beautiful quality is flushed down the drain, and then allow a recording to go out on the market that is a poor substitute for what she is. That's just plain wrong."

Vickers's long-standing animosity for Solti dates from

those *Aïda* sessions in Rome, and the tenor makes no bones that his allegiance is to Herbert von Karajan, the conductor with whom he most enjoys singing. "There is no question Karajan stands head and shoulders above every conductor in the world today. He's very hard to work with, to be sure, but only because he demands an incredible standard for music's sake. This is especially terrifying to me because he believes I am much better than I believe I am. He pushes me to the ultimate every moment, so I am on my knuckle whenever I sing with him. There are very few things in my profession and life that get to me emotionally and put me in a position to be hurt. I am not emotionally the Met, or Covent Garden, or Scala, or Salzburg. I *am* emotionally Karajan, and if he chose to do so, he could cut me to ribbons; he knows it. But that kind of relationship is rare in the music world.

"When a man stands as high as Karajan and sets such a standard, when his grasp and his ability and his mind are so great, he cannot help but produce enemies. It is one of the sad things about the heart of mankind. The jealousy and the envy this man is a victim of absolutely horrifies me, for he is a great, great human being. I met him first in 1957 in an audition. I didn't get halfway through my aria when he called me offstage and said, 'Let's do *Tristan* together next year.' 'Don't be crazy,' I said. 'I'm not ready for *Tristan*.' 'Why not?' 'I'm too young.' 'Never mind, one day you will be my Tristan.' Today I am.

"I must tell you, however, I never thought I would be, because I am not a Wagner fan. *Parsifal* I accept, I love. But apart from *Parsifal,* the one really great work Wagner wrote was *The Flying Dutchman*. The rest I don't go for. Perhaps it is again my background, but I can't stand Wagner's colossal arrogance, and I hate his philosophy with a passion. When I began to delve seriously into

*Tristan,* it became a real battle; the more I studied it, the less I wanted to sing the role. In a way, this may have been the best thing that could have happened to me from the standpoint of performing the part. It made it all the more easy to stay outside the music and drama emotionally and project what the work is really about.

"You see, if a singer is successful in moving the public, it is because he has done his homework, not because he has become profoundly involved in the emotions of a situation. If you go the latter route, your voice will not survive, you interfere with your own technique. As a youngster I always performed only for myself; I believe all young singers are that way. That's why they don't project as an old, experienced horse like myself does. As you grow older and develop a real knowledge of what you are all about, you become less and less emotionally involved in what you do; you reach an audience without exhausting yourself.

"I do admit before singing *Tristan* a sort of weariness comes over me. I have the same sensation—if you can imagine it—of loading a big truck with gravel. I know that's a terrible parallel to make, but it is the sort of fatigue I would have after loading that truck. When I go to the theater, I know from the moment I sit down at my makeup table until I get dressed to go home after the performance it will be about seven-and-one-half hours. That's a long, long evening. It's not a question of nerves. I can't say I ever really get nervous, though I sometimes have twinges of nerves just before I go on in the second act. Everyone thinks the third act of *Tristan* is the tough one, but the second act is the really difficult one for a tenor. The third is heavy, long, and demanding, but it's the exposure of the second act and the vocal technique it demands that's the stickler.

"My wife gets furious at me when I say I don't like

Wagner because she feels any work of art is above its philosophy, in the case of Wagner, above the philosophy of Nietzsche, beyond the autobiographical aspects of *Tristan*. You see, I believe Wagner wrote *Tristan* as a defense of his own immorality; it is not just a love story. My wife, who is very interested in the background preparation of my roles, felt much as I did while I was studying the role, but when she witnessed the thing onstage, she was completely overcome by the experience of this dying man, who by the power of his love willed Isolde to him. She felt Tristan was any lonely, dying soldier on a battlefield. But I maintain this is one of the diabolical qualities of *Tristan;* the power, the genius of Wagner, the beauty of the music convinces you that wrong is right. He does this in the first act of *Die Walküre* as well. He convinces you it is all right for Siegmund to have a love affair with his sister."

It was the dramatic premise rather than anything vocal which put Vickers off *Tristan* for so long. But he finally performed the opera in Buenos Aires in 1971. His Isolde on that occasion was Birgit Nilsson. Like Karajan, she had long urged him to sing Tristan. When Vickers at last relented, Nilsson wrote him a charming letter in which she said that she now understood how Jacob felt after waiting fourteen years for Rachel. Many critics have written that Vickers is the long-awaited heir to the late Lauritz Melchior, the greatest of Tristans. But Vickers refuses to accept this. "I believe there has been no successor to Melchior because our day and age put too great an emphasis on being youthful, and young singers in this time of the jet, and given the immediate exposure of success, have been tempted to leap into Melchior's roles before they were ready. A lot of tenors, who are going to remain nameless, have gone down the drain recently for no other reason than they took on Tristan and Siegfried before they should have.

"The great Melchior sang as a baritone until he was nearly thirty. It wasn't until after that, that he began to sing the dramatic tenor parts. I suspect he was about my age when he sang Tristan. And remember, too, Martinelli never opened the score of *Otello* until he was past fifty. But once you are mature and have entered the dramatic repertory, you still have to be very careful. Many people think that if you're a Wagner tenor, you're a Wagner tenor. I don't believe it. I think the Wagnerian tenor roles fall into two distinct categories. Ideally one group is Tristan, Siegmund, Parsifal, and maybe Erik. The other group consists of Lohengrin, Tannhäuser, Walther in *Meistersinger*, and the young Siegfried. Now the older Siegfried should fall into the group with Tristan, not the other group, but anyone who sings Siegfried—and it's not going to be me—sings both the young and the old.

"The parts in the first group are true dramatic tenor roles, really heavy stuff. The others are, to my mind, the German equivalent of Italian spinto parts. Now, Melchior did sing *Tannhäuser* and *Lohengrin*, but he was never really at his best in either; *Lohengrin*, especially, was too lyric for him. And he never sang *Meistersinger* at all. That was really too lyric, and he couldn't manage it; he was a wise old codger.

"Take Verdi as well. Because you can sing *La Forza del Destino*, which I will do, or *Aïda*, doesn't mean you should sing Alfredo, though some tenors have mixed these roles. Personally, I don't want to hear a *Trovatore* voice in *Traviata*. If there is real artistry and an ability to sing lyrically, I can take a *Trovatore* voice in *Ballo*. I am a fairly heavy tenor, but I enjoy singing *Ballo*. The romantic aspects of it allow you to use real *espressivo* and mezza voce, and the heroics of a voice like mine go well with the manly character of Riccardo. The question, however, is actually not as acute in Verdi as it is in Wagner, because whatever you sing by Verdi massages your voice; Wagner uses it ruthlessly."

This categorizing of tenor types is something the layman is not aware of. To most, a tenor is a tenor. Vickers feels that even a professional like Berlioz was guilty of the misunderstanding. "The reason *The Trojans* is such a challenge is that Berlioz did not write Aeneas for one voice, but four. His first entrance is music for an Italian spinto, but the second—the scene with Hector's ghost—is actually for a lyric baritone! Then comes the third entrance, and it is big heroic-tenor singing, *Otello* stuff. Finally, there is the Garden Scene, and it calls for a lyric tenor, a Beniamino Gigli kind of a voice. Somehow, if you sing Aeneas, you have to be a composite of all these types. I have to make a compromise for Aeneas with my basically dramatic voice. If I let it go too much in the heroic sections, I'll be in trouble in the lyric scenes. But, if I stifle the lyricism, I'll cramp myself up so that I can't let go in the big scenes. Together with this is the problem of the tessitura, or the positioning of a melody in the voice. This is often ungrateful in Berlioz."

Though the reputation of most singers is built today on the operatic, not the concert, stage, Vickers is one of the few who is equally at home in these two diverse realms. By his own admission, he doesn't do as much concert work as he would like, and he talks longingly of performing more Bach and Handel. It is unprecedented for a man famous for Otello and Tristan to possess the training and facility to command as well the tenor solos in *Messiah*. Yet, it was Vickers's recording of the latter with Sir Thomas Beecham

Jon Vickers (*Photo by Erika Davidson*)

which first introduced his voice to many in the United States.

"When my management called me and said they had a request from Sir Thomas for that recording, I said 'But he's never heard me.' 'Oh, yes he has; he heard you sing Handel's *Samson* at Covent Garden.' 'Well,' I said, 'I am happy to do the recording, but I just don't think he is going to accept me as a tenor for the *Messiah*.' Anyway, I went along to the first rehearsal, and as luck would have it I bumped into Sir Thomas in a doorway. I introduced myself and said 'It's a great honor for me to be working with you.' 'Ohhhh,' he said, 'It's a great honor for me to be working with *you*.' I laughed at that and said, 'But I am also apprehensive to be working with you.' 'Ohhhh,' he countered, 'but I am apprehensive to be working with *you*.' 'Now listen,' I said, 'We're not going to get anywhere unless you be serious.' Well, he quipped some more and then I tried to explain why I thought he would never accept me for the *Messiah*. 'First of all, Sir Thomas, I'm not an English tenor.' 'THANK GOD,' he roared. Then I said, 'I do not conceive the first recitative, "Comfort ye," or the aria "Every valley" as a watered-down idea of a long-bearded man in the sky patting the children of Israel gently on the head saying "Now, now, be good people." I envision this as the impassioned prophet Isaiah, standing on a hillside commanding the people to "Comfort ye"; God's promises are that "Every valley shall be exalted and every mountain and hill made low."

" 'That's very interesting,' Sir Thomas said. 'Come on, let's do it right now with the orchestra.' Cold, like that, bang! He took me to the podium and said to the engineers, 'We'll take this one.' Then to me he said, 'Don't pay any attention to me. Go on, just sing it.' I did. After hearing the playback he said, 'That's wonderful, but these orchestrations don't suit your sound at all. I'll take them back to Eugene Goossens and have them redone for you.' And he had all my parts reorchestrated. Later he was slammed by the critics for the orchestrations, not just of my solos but of the whole piece, and perhaps they do go a bit too far. But in their way they are no worse than the people who are making money through the gimmick of the *Messiah* in a so-called 'pure' state. They dig out all this nauseating, dry material and shove it back into the work, along with their baroque organs and the rest of it. But the best orchestration of the *Messiah* was done by no less than Mozart. If you study the monumental approach of Mozart's orchestrations for Handel's music, you realize Mozart had a greater view of the *Messiah* than did Handel.

"But even Mozart himself is prey to the 'purists.' They try to make us think of him as a piece of Dresden china that we must handle with exceeding care lest he break. Sir Thomas always said it was a German economist who cooked up the idea of 'ideal' Mozart. This enabled opera managers to hire small voices at lower fees and produce 'ideal' Mozart for less money. Sir Thomas always used an orchestra of not less than eighty for Mozart. But again the critics slammed him for it, as they did me when I sang 'Il mio tesoro' from *Don Giovanni* in concert. I would love to sing all of Don Ottavio, but my voice and approach are not the popular way. The public might accept Ottavio as a more manly figure, but the critics would never.

"Anyway, Sir Thomas and I got along marvelously. I loved working with him and had only one difficult moment. He got a bee in his bonnet about the way I said 'valley.' I could see him getting uptight about it, and finally he said 'It is not val-lee, Mr. Vickers, it's val-lay.' 'Well, Sir Thomas,'

I replied, 'You're just going to have to put up with my vulgar American accent. You see in Canada and the United States we think of a val-lee as something between two hills. But a val-lay is someone who helps you get dressed.' He roared with laughter. 'Don't tell me, Mr. Vickers, that you are not a true tenor, that you wouldn't exalt your val-lay!' There was never another word said about it after that."

Vickers's recitals have been too few for one so sensitively attuned to the song literature. He feels strongly, however, that it is too difficult to operate with freedom on the recital stage today. "The field is pretty much dead. It has to do with the community concert approach operated by Columbia Artists Management. This involves package deals in which one good artist, or one passé artist, is used to sell a lot of second- and third-rate artists. If you don't take the second-rate stuff, you don't get the first-rate. The public has gotten sick of paying to hear second-rate performers, and the concert field in America has been hurt as a result.

"There is also the phenomenon of the big opera star who is engaged for a shortish program of potboilers and arias. I won't be a party to that. I believe the concert field is a great opportunity for making music and its repertory is limitless. If I go onto the concert stage, I insist on going as a concert and not an operatic artist. I've been criticized because I won't sing a string of arias. Frankly, very few arias stand up out of context. They sound and feel dismembered to me. The orchestral texture is missing, and no matter how good an accompanist you have, he can't make up for the loss. Because I won't compromise on this, a lot of organizations who hire opera singers are not interested in me. To tell the truth, I'm not interested in them either."

Whether in concert or opera, to Vickers every performance is different from the last because a singer never feels the same way twice. "You're affected by climatic conditions, whether the air-conditioning is on or off—and I hope to heaven it's off—and many other little things have a profound effect on the vocal mechanism. Then there's your mental state. You begin to think 'How am I going to be vocally?' for, despite the emphasis I place on interpretation, if the voice does not convey the dramatic impact of the music, no one will accept your interpretation. The voice is fundamental, though I do decry the opera star who feels voice is all-important. It's important only insofar as it functions as an instrument to convey your ideas. A voice is a means of communication, and if it doesn't work, I can't communicate. This is always the last thing in my mind before I present myself to the public.

"It's crazy that someone's entire life and livelihood should depend upon two silly things stuck in his windpipe. We invest three or four months learning a big opera, then we rehearse for four or five weeks. Our colleagues are depending upon us, and suddenly we realize we are coming down with a cold. We go to a doctor, tell him a cold is coming and he says 'So what?' Well, of course, you can say that to anyone, a secretary or another doctor. After all, a doctor can put on a surgical mask and go on, can't he? But we have those two blessed little things in our throat, and we can't go on unless they feel right."

It is rare to find a singer who doesn't at some point in a career experience a vocal problem or crisis of some sort. Jon Vickers is no exception. "A few years back, about 1963, I had a bit of a vocal crisis—not serious, but serious enough to send me back to Mr. Lambert who was still alive at the time. I told him I had a problem, and he said 'I know, I heard it on the last Met broadcast.' 'Now others hadn't noticed it, but he had. For a month he made me sing nothing but Handel, Mozart, and Bach, and he would not allow me to talk from day to day; talking is just terrible on a singer's throat, and I do try to cut back on needless talking. There are a lot of other limitations for singers as well. I take lots of vitamin C; I don't go in public places, not even to the movies; and I always use taxis—public transport would just be asking for trouble. In short, I become a hermit.

"A hotel room to me is a prison. It's the place I go willingly or unwillingly to preserve the energy needed for my work. I remove myself from society; unfortunately, I remove myself from my family as well. So a hotel room for me is not the glamorous place many think. Many also believe an opera singer lives in high society. Maybe some do. If so, if they are members of the jet set, it is to their detriment and ultimate downfall. An opera singer, I am convinced, must first think of himself as an artist. If he compromises this to be with the wealthy, with people of position, he is going to sap his strength and can no longer function as an artist. So travel becomes solitary confinement. Just because it is voluntary doesn't make it any easier.

"People say to me, 'How fortunate you are to go about the world, be in the major cities.' I always think of the great Kirsten Flagstad, who was once asked what she would do when she retired. 'Well, I think I'll knit awhile and then travel.' 'Why travel?' she was asked. 'Because I haven't seen anything.' Now Flagstad had sung everywhere, but she had realized that she had to cut herself off from things a tourist does because these would exhaust her as an artist. We travel for the job, and for the most part, an opera singer is a lonely person. If there is one thing all singers must learn to cope with, it is personal loneliness. This is intensified by the enormous contrast between the stage and the hotel room. We stand onstage, interpret our roles, rip our emotions wide open, and are exceedingly sensitive to every influence. If you've been a success, there is a tremendous sense of unity between yourself and everyone involved in the performance. Then, you scrape off your makeup, have a shower, sign some autographs, and suddenly it's all over. You are just another person in a big city, in a strange place where your only home is a hotel room.

"Remember, too, we can sing only until about fifty, so we have to make our life's earnings in a period of fifteen years, because you don't—or I certainly didn't—break even until you are thirty-five. We have no sick pay, no pension schemes, no retirement plans. It's one thing to point an accusing finger at a young singer trying to get ahead and become established, but I ache for young singers more today than I ached for myself at their age. It is much more difficult today for a singer than when I began. I would die at the thought of one of my children trying to start as a singer now. They would have heinous obstacles to overcome.

"And, with all due respect to those past fifty who are still singing, I don't want to hear them, nor do I want people to hear me past that age. I had hoped to bow out of opera at forty-seven, but that wasn't possible. I still think fifty remains a possibility. There are many in the profession urging me to go on until sixty, and there are those who smile and say, 'You'll never be able to give it up; you'll be miserable.' But I think I have more personal resources than that. I am convinced I could give it up—and when I do, I will get right out of it. I don't want any part of production or of teaching. I have flirted with the idea of conducting, and I can just hear people saying, 'Oh my God, here comes another one.' But I don't think I'm being silly, for I have no ambition to be a conductor of any stature.

I feel if I went back to the conservatory and studied for two or three years that I have enough music in me, enough experience and a wealth of accumulated knowledge, that I might be able to give something to a place like Edmonton, Halifax, Calgary, or even Winnipeg. If this isn't possible, I would love to have a choral society, a Bach group. If you look back across my life and realize that I have worked successfully with men like Karajan, Serafin, Beecham, Knappertsbusch, Klemperer, Böhm, Kempe, Reiner, Bernstein, Kubelik, and Giulini—and I could go on and on—I must have learned something from these great musicians and have something to share."

Vickers is only a few years short of the deadline he has set for ending his career, and already the tenor is booked up to his fiftieth birthday in 1976. He is asked more and more for the most dramatic and demanding roles in the tenor repertory. In the 1973–74 season at the Metropolitan Opera alone, he sang Aeneas, Otello, and Tristan. This must bother him, for such continued emphasis on so heavy a repertory will shorten his singing life and make the fifty cut-off point truly a reality. The pressure on him to sing everywhere is as great as it is understandable. As Chapin puts it: "It is very hard for the Met, as it is for any company, to get the great artists to spend sufficient time with you. If Jon should turn around one day and say, 'I'll give you six months,' I would faint, and after I had recovered I'd make damn certain we kept him busy and happy for the six months. But I'll take what I can get, and the more the merrier, particularly with an artist like Jon. He never gets out on the stage without giving the public what they have come to see and hear. I am also a firm believer that an intellectual artist—and Jon certainly is in that category— knows best what they can do, knows the moment when they are ready to move into new repertory. Hopefully, we can move with them, change as their dramatic interest goes into other areas. Simply stated, if Jon Vickers came to me and said he would like to do *Mother Goose,* I would be very much inclined to mount a production of *Mother Goose* for him."

Doubling the problems and pressures facing every performing artist today is jet travel, which allows one to pop from city to city. This leads to an "If it's Tuesday, it must be *Carmen*" sort of existence. Jon Vickers is one of the few singers who keeps a governor on himself, who has learned to say no and mean it. He allows ample time to get away from his career and get back to the farm, to the barns that need cleaning, the fields that need plowing. Here, he belies the concept of what an opera star is and how he behaves.

Jon Vickers as Florestan in Beethoven's *Fidelio* (*Photo by Louis Mélançon*)

"I have quite a nice workshop in the basement of my garage, and I love to do woodwork. I carried out the major part of our kitchen alterations and built my sons' bunk beds, desks, and closets. Besides that, I like to golf and occasionally I get my skis on. I'm not much for the water or swimming, though I wish I could be as athletic as I was when I was young. I hate the feeling of not having the opportunity to use my muscles more often. However, I don't want to put too much emphasis on the physical side of things, because there is more to my life away from the stage. We have a beautiful library, and I do a considerable amount of reading. It forms a large portion of my enjoyment and is also an active part of my career, as I read on transatlantic flights and in hotels.

"I have been reading a lot of Paul Tillich lately, and also in the area they call process-thought religion. I've tried to get hold of literature that's good about the rise of the Mao regime in China, but, as you can imagine, it's skimpy at the moment. I'm fascinated by communism, though I have no sympathy for it at all. I suppose it fascinates me in the same way I would be fascinated by a black widow spider. Communism is a vicious, dangerous thing in the world today, a great creeping cancer. I'm also still active in church life, as I have been since I was a little boy. That's a natural inheritance from my parents. I've never lost my deep religious convictions, my Christian faith. I love the church, though not necessarily all those connected with it. But still, the church is worth working for."

The most vital thing, however, in Vickers's life is his family, a subject the very private person within him balks at discussing. "I have tried to become what I call a conscious schizophrenic, in order to keep my personal life and my professional life totally separated. Even when I talk about myself in interviews, I have the feeling I'm talking about someone else. I know what the interviewer is trying to do —he's doing his utmost to find the real person in me, and I am consciously allowing him just those peeks I want him to see and desperately trying to protect my family, for my first responsibility is certainly not to my career, but to my family. The result, of course, is this feeling of talking about someone else. To a degree this is explicable, because onstage I'm constantly being someone else. I am not Jon Vickers there, but Otello, Tristan, or Canio, all the various personalities I have learned to become. So it is not difficult to prevent you from getting a full look at the real me.

"I will tell you that I have five children—two daughters and three sons. My eldest daughter is just entering the university, my eldest son is going into his last year of high school, and my youngest is about eight. I try to make them happy kids, and I am determined that as they grow up, they think of me only as their dad. I don't want them to think of me as some kind of celebrity, whatever that means, because if they do, they might start thinking of themselves as mini-celebrities. I have had sufficient experience in this profession to have seen children made very confused because they have been utilized to enhance a parent's propaganda.

"Of course, I'm not so all-fired idealistic as I might sound. There is probably a good deal of selfishness in my attitude, because I am determined I must have a haven of refuge from my professional life. That's why I have chosen to live in the country, to shun the press. Nearly all artists know that to be effective in our jobs, we have to remove ourselves from the scene and recharge ourselves emotionally and spiritually. The Wagner family named their house *Wahnfried*, meaning roughly 'Freedom from madness.' My home is my freedom from madness. This is what keeps my feet on the ground, keeps my mental and spiritual balance. Not only do the kids think of me only as their dad, I think of myself as only their dad."

# Franco Corelli

BY

*Joan Downs*

FRANCO CORELLI speaks very little English. The homeliest words ride the edge of consciousness, beckon seductively, finally elude him. His conversation is a cryptic Anglo-Italian mosaic that translates imperfectly in either tongue. *"Stupido,"* he denounces himself over and over as his right foot taps an impatient tattoo against the table leg. But on a pale winter afternoon as Corelli sits in the shadows relaxing in his favorite chair and listening to a recording of Caruso singing "Di quella pira," his foot grows still, his eyes begin to shine, and a shy smile plays at the corners of his mouth. When the music stops, the words tumble out, in lucid, lyrical, very nearly grammatical profusion.

"I don't say I am an artist. That would not be modest. But I can say that I feel like an artist, I suffer like an artist. I remember the first time music opened her doors to me. I was ten and visiting a church in a neighboring town. It was very still and when the organ's sad voice began to resonate through the silence, I could hear such suffering trapped inside the melody I felt myself go empty inside. Sometimes, in the opera house, I can forget myself and go inside a role. It happens on a night when the conductor hypnotizes the orchestra so that they feel only his eyes and arms. On that night they play with a mighty sound and the music goes inside me. I can feel it pierce my heart. My eyes fill with tears. In that moment I am absolutely fragile, and when I sing my heart is full of melody."

By any standards, Franco Corelli is a superstar. He has a large robust voice of exceptional power and splendid timbre that can flood a theater, thrilling the audience with a sensuous grace that is entirely masculine. He is also a man addicted to western films because cowboys are the only men in America who are strong enough to cry, a man who despite critical rebuke cannot choke the sob from Rodolfo's voice as Mimì gasps her final breath. Critics may chide his Italianate sob and lingering highs; audiences adore him. Operagoers, quick to spot a phony, recognize in Corelli's unabashed outpouring of emotions a man whose definition of himself is indivisible from his music.

It is a success story unprecedented in the history of opera or in any press agent's fairy tale. Virtually self-taught, from the germ of a start winning a local amateur singing contest and with scarcely any indulgence in trial runs with minor roles in secondary opera houses, Corelli blazed a trail, sensational as a comet, straight to the top of international opera. Less than two years after his opera debut, he was singing opposite Maria Callas, then *prima donna del mondo*. Twenty years later Corelli has opened more seasons and

Franco Corelli at the Arena di Verona, Italy (*Photo by Erika Davidson*)

played more roles in more opera houses than any other tenor in his time. At a reported $10,000 an appearance, combined with the fruits of his knack for investing—his tax consultant annually demands four weeks of his time—Corelli's income hovers in the middle six figures and he is quite possibly the richest tenor in the world.

There is little doubt that his career was facilitated in the beginning by the powerful extramusical advantage of enormous good looks, Provocatively clad in clinging velvet tights, Corelli's shapely legs earned the accolade *"Coscia d'Oro"*—"Golden Calves"—from Milanese opera buffs. Soon enough he would plead with critics to forget about reviewing his legs and concentrate instead on his music—"It's hard enough to keep your voice in shape without having to worry about your figure," he would say—but in fact the protest which he registered for many years was often *sotto voce*. In the early years in Italy when Corelli sang Pierre Bezukhov in a San Carlo production of *War and Peace*, the role called for a fat man wearing spectacles. Following two days of persuasion Corelli consented to make up properly for the role—but once he got onstage he slipped the glasses into his coat pocket. In the United States before the Metropolitan Opera's revival of *Turandot*, Corelli amused his colleagues by complaining that Cecil Beaton's costumes did not taper sufficiently at the waist. In truth he rarely missed an opportunity to capitalize on his comely appearance.

Who could blame him. Puccini's most winsome melodies could not disguise the overstuffed reality of Bjoerling's smile wreathed in chins or the comical shadow cast by Caruso's squat frame. Corelli's tall (six-feet-one), dark presence had an electrifying effect on audiences. For the first time they could believe that here was a man worthy of the devotion of the haughty Oriental Princess Turandot or the beauteous Ethiopian slave Aïda.

The leading ladies were hardly more immune. Callas, grateful to find one singing partner she did not tower over, frankly told Corelli that one strong argument favoring his selection to appear with her in *La Vestale* was that he had the proper physique for a Roman centurion. "When I have a fat little tenor next to me," sighed Antonietta Stella, "obviously I cannot get inspired. In *Trovatore* when I sing 'Sei tu dal ciel discesco' ['It is he descended from heaven'] with Franco, one really feels he has descended from heaven. Most of the other tenors could have dropped down from anywhere."

Even at the executive offices at the Metropolitan, commenting on the aphrodisiacal powers of a tenor, then General Manager Rudolf Bing said, "The tenor with a secure top exerts a sexual fascination on people, not just women, men too. The best tenor has a quality, a timbre, that's essentially a sexual stimulant—that is why they are so highly paid."

Bing was so convinced of a tenor's importance to the success of an operatic production that, according to Corelli, during one especially severe epidemic of multiple cancellations, the steely autocrat of the Met was literally brought to his knees. Determined to fill yet another vacancy in his evening lineup of heroes, Bing unexpectedly appeared at Corelli's midtown Manhattan apartment one morning where he was admitted by a maid. His host was still asleep. Hearing a rap at his bedroom door, the unsuspecting tenor arose and, still in his rumpled pajamas, opened the door to the astonishing vision of the future peer of the realm kneeling prayerfully at his feet. Only when Corelli had consented to sing at five consecutive performances did Bing rise. Later, the crisis past, Bing remarked, "Nobody is irreplaceable in the opera house. But," he conceded, "Franco is more irreplaceable than the others."

Nevertheless, a romantic aura cannot sustain a singer's place in opera's panoply of superstars. The era is past of the opera house as a showcase for ladies dewy in diamonds preening among the bright plumage of French silks and sumptuous brocades. At $20.00 for a seat in the orchestra, to most people an evening at the opera can no longer be a familiar pleasure, but one for which they prepare themselves to receive a grand reaction. A tenor's longevity is directly linked with his effectiveness in producing emotion in the listener. Gorgeous sound is what they come to hear: Corelli's bold old-fashioned brand of vocalism with its penetrating low tones and full clarion C's that evoke the lyrical simplicity of Puccini and that make the triumphal scene of Verdi's *Aïda* a definition of triumph.

Inevitably there was an occasional snag to mar the fledgling artist's bounding success. In a 1957 performance of *Pagliacci* in Milan he sang so poorly the exasperated conductor flung down his baton and buried his face in the score, abruptly abandoning the novice tenor to his own devices. With the opera's fatal closing words "La commedia è finita"—"the comedy is ended"—the curtain descended in a blizzard of whistles. The next morning scooping up his tattered pride the crestfallen young singer tried to cancel all his remaining contracts. Wisely, the opera house refused.

"I was so ashamed," Corelli winces. Then the excuses begin: "I ate some salami and late in the afternoon I began to have a pain in my liver. That night my head began to spin and my stomach—" he pauses, then resumes, his jaw set firmly. "It was a bad performance," he admits quietly. "I was one bar ahead of the conductor all evening.

Every moment I was afraid. When I was at the start of my career, do you know what thought ran through my mind the moment I stepped onstage? I hoped I would arrive at the end of the opera. I prayed that I would have the strength to sing every note, that I would be onstage when the final curtain fell." Only when he became confident that he would give a complete performance could Corelli concern himself with interpretation of the score. And then a new problem arose. "I discovered where the music said *mezza voce*—sing softly—there was an uneasiness in the middle of my voice. Until my voice was educated, I could not carry out the score's instructions. For me, negotiating the E–F passage can still be tricky."

In the early years he aimed at swelling volumes and little else, Corelli confides, and the result was often monochromatic and inexpressive. He thinks at times he may have fooled the audience, but never himself. "Many mornings I woke up depressed. I would work for fifteen days on a score and on the sixteenth day my voice would stumble again in exactly the same passages. When I sang *Poliuto* I had a great deal of difficulty, and one day when my voice refused to go any further I became so frustrated, I lost all control. I began screaming and before I knew what I was doing I had smashed the music rack on the piano. One of the hardest lessons for me to learn was that the muscle cannot be forced, the throat is commanded by the brain."

It took nine years of vocalizing for Corelli's throat to become flexible and his ear to grow keen enough to place the voice properly. Two-thirds of that time was on-the-job training. In a matter of three years, recalcitrant center and all, his voice had catapulted him from first honors in a spring music festival, in which he sang "Celeste Aïda" (the only aria he knew), to the stages of the world's major opera houses. "I said to myself, you don't know much about singing," he recalls with a sheepish smile directed at youthful understatement.

Determined to learn everything, despite his family's unsympathetic attitude regarding his musical aspirations, Corelli embarked on an intensive do-it-yourself program. He bought every book he could find on singing and opera—he estimates a thousand—countless recordings by reigning tenors of the past, and, perhaps the most valuable investment of all—a tape recorder. "My friendly spy," he calls it, "it always tells the truth." Since 1955 Corelli has taped all of his performances and rehearsals, analyzing them meticulously the following day. "I began to know the worst about my voice," he grimaces, "and to learn to think about singing."

For Corelli the major defects of his instrument were an inability to sing pianissimo and to project tones that were round as well as ringing. Oddly enough, one deficiency that did not particularly worry him was an initially narrow range. In fact he sang for several years before he had a high C, a rather singular handicap for a musician rapidly gaining in reputation as one of the world's leading tenors. But if Corelli knew little about molding a phrase, he understood very well his own physical capacities, a legacy of the days when he was a superb athlete. "I did not have the complete extension of my voice," he says, "and I didn't force it. I knew that would be the beginning of the end of my voice. After six years the high C came."

Today Corelli's three-octave range extends from C below middle C to high C. At home when he vocalizes sometimes he can touch high E-flat and, for the record, when he and Joan Sutherland sang *Les Huguenots* (in Italian at La Scala) he sang a D-natural. "At the end of the first act of *Trovatore*,

I could take a C-sharp, but I always put on the D-flat," he
allows himself a brief display of pride. "On a piano they are
the same note. But with the voice, as with any stringed
instrument, they are two different sounds. D-flat has an extra
vibration—you can hear it and the singer can feel it. For the
repertory I sing, however, the top note I need is C."

No stranger would ever guess from hearing Corelli's
speaking voice that he earns his living as a singer. Although
no longer concerned about the once elusive high C, the
fiery cape-and-sword adventurer of the stage lives in fear,
endlessly worrying about his vocal condition. As a result,
offstage his voice resembles the male equivalent of a Jackie
Onassis whisper, although sometimes it takes on a thin
granitic quality that makes one long to request that he clear
his throat. (On other occasions he clears his throat dozens
of times in the space of an hour until it seems certain he
must have grated his tonsils raw.) However, he has one
of the healthiest larynxes in the business: since 1954 he
has had to suspend fewer than a dozen performances.

"The tenor voice is special, less natural for a man than
the baritone or a bass, and requires much attention," Corelli
confirms. "But," he admits ruefully, "I live on nerves. Someone told me it is a good thing for an artist to have nerves
—otherwise he sounds mechanical. Ninety-nine percent of
all artists get nervous; for me, however, sometimes I think
I am 99 percent nerves." Years ago, following a foolhardy
nonstop six-month bout of vocalizing, Corelli lost the top
of his register for four months. Later, when he was singing
*Carmen* in Enna, Sicily, his voice broke and he could not
continue, a waking nightmare whose memory haunts him
today.

"Some day," Corelli says soberly, "it will all be over. I
will get up and know that the voice is no longer beautiful.

I will stop. Never will I present an audience with a moment of pity," he vows. Clenching his fist, he scowls dramatically, calling attention to the triangular scar that indents his forehead and the broken nose that save his face from pretty boy perfection. Briefly he is distracted. "Last night I was up until three o'clock with an aching tooth," the consequence of catch-as-catch-can dentistry in a peripatetic life that has him three months here, four weeks there, he explains. Pulling his faded blue terry cloth robe tight, he strides up and down the center of the room, an imaginary ice bag pressed to his cheek. "Then today I had to sing the matinee of *Bohème,* and my throat hurt and my jaw was stiff. When the curtain went up I wasn't sure I would be able to open my mouth." Still, he looks as if he could swallow a basketball without much trouble.

Corelli's preperformance routine has hardly altered in the last fifteen years and very much resembles that of other opera singers. The day before he is scheduled to sing he tries not to speak. He used to communicate with his wife by passing notes, but now he says that is no longer necessary. "After sixteen years of marriage she knows what is in my mind—sometimes too much." He cannot attend concerts by other singers for fear of raising sympathetic spasms in his own throat. A nightly tranquilizer does not free him from the insomnia which has plagued him all his life, although it enables him to stop worrying about being awake. Often he gets up for a nocturnal study session listening for his own vocal flaws in the tape of his last rehearsal.

As on most mornings, the day of a performance Corelli sleeps until noon—apparently Morpheus appears with Aurora—then begins his day with fifty push-ups. The old chestnut of the singer-athlete has more legitimacy than the layman may suspect. The exertion of each performance claims three to four pounds of Corelli's sturdy 205-pound frame, as it probably does from most of his colleagues. He gains it back within an hour following the last act, however. "I retain water, and I drink it by the quart. I really like it better than wine," he claims. His voice does not imperil his wife's Baccarat goblets: "No voice is strong enough to break glass," Corelli dismisses the antique myth while spinning the stem speculatively in his fingers. "The vibrations roam freely in the air and before the crystal shattered, the tympanum of the ear would burst." Nevertheless, without a solid girdle of muscle supporting his diaphragm, he could not fill his forty-seven-inch chest with enough air to provide the lung power necessary to spin out the long unbroken line of his legato in Cavaradossi's poignant lament "E lucevan le stelle" when he sings *Tosca,* or in Andrea Chénier's farewell poem from prison, "Come un bel dì di maggio."

Franco Corelli as Andrea Chénier in the Giordano opera (*Photo by Erio Piccagliani*)

The remainder of the day is occupied in watching television and in lubricating his throat with occasional draughts from a steaming mug of tea laced with honey "to give me strength." If the weather is mild, submerged in a voluminous camel's hair coat, his throat swathed in a thick muffler, he may take Pipi, his toy gray poodle, for a walk in Central Park. "The climate in America is treacherous," contends Corelli. "In Italy from October to April the weather is cool; from May to September it is warm. Here in New York in December one day it's fifty or sixty degrees, the next morning it's nineteen degrees." On one of the former, a sixty-one-degree day in mid-February 1974, Corelli managed to avoid the watchful eye of his wife, who is even more vigilant concerning his health than he, and leave the apartment without his scarf. The next morning he awoke with a sore throat, by afternoon he had a raging fever, and at nightfall the doctor came to give him an injection of antibiotics, as he would for the following five nights. Maybe he has taken to good care of his throat, the tenor conjectured a week later when it was still inflamed and he was forced to cancel his holiday in Italy. Is it possible that years of pampering can lower a singer's resistance so that his ability to fight infection is actually impaired?

Two hours before curtain time Corelli warms up with some mild vocal exercises, singing brief quotes from his role at one-quarter voice. As the time draws near for him to dress to leave for the theater, his face grows taut and a muscle twitches in his neck, commencing a neural mutiny that erupts in the teeth-rattling, leg-trembling fear that grips him before he sings. "I am never happy when I sing," he asserts convincingly. "Maybe when I'm shaving."

When finally he does drag himself onstage, his concentration screens out all but the business at hand. Once, when

he was performing *Carmen* in the open air arena in Verona,
a storm blew up over the city during the second act. With
scenery crashing down all around him, the horrified audience implored the hapless Don José, "Get off, get off!"
Immersed in the music, Corelli sang on, oblivious to the
commotion of man and elements, until finally the artistic
director dragged him offstage—still singing at the top of
his lungs.

"That music makes your blood race, makes you alive, and
for me the Arena di Verona is the best theater in the world
because you can see a spectacle within a spectacle," declares
Corelli, his eyes flashing. "From three o'clock in the afternoon people begin arriving in the piazza, coming from Hol-
land, Sweden, England, Germany, and France. By eight
o'clock twenty-five thousand people are seated in the arena
and you can hear a breath. That day it had rained all afternoon and I had to perform with no rehearsal. When I
entered the arena and saw twenty-five thousand people, my
heart inside me exploded cannonballs. I felt no larger than
a fly and all I could wonder was how will they hear my
voice."

Giving Pipi a final good-bye pat, Loretta Corelli hands
her coat to her husband with an air of determination. It is
seven-thirty. A steady stream of men and women in evening
clothes is passing through the gates of the great hall of the
Metropolitan, but the tenor of the evening is still being
coaxed into the limousine waiting at the curb outside his
57th Street apartment house. "I did not choose or look for
this life, it was fate," he moans, repeating a familiar lament,
invariably accompanied by a large theatrical frown. But
the tremor in his knees is genuine. Mrs. Corelli nods be-
nignly.

At three minutes before eight, Corelli stands stiffly in

front of his dressing room mirror smartly turned out in a fitted violet frock coat, dove gray trousers, and a waist-hugging black velvet vest. As the cosmetician lightly sprays his collar-length black wavy hair (he rarely wears a wig), Corelli peers into the glass inspecting his face. For Corelli, makeup is more than an accessory; he builds his character from the outside in—"like Carol Burnett," whom he greatly admires. Probably closer to the heart of the matter, however, is Corelli's superstition that he can predict the success of a performance by how well his makeup goes on. If he looks like Rodolfo, he will sing like Rodolfo—"with tender warmth." *"Molto vanitoso"* ("Very vain"), laughs Loretta Corelli.

Walking to the wings, he snaps on a tape recorder behind the backstage intercom. Then spotting a violinist from the orchestra he calls, "How is it tonight?" Some nights, Corelli explains, his high C must be higher than others. "Many maestros have written about this problem. In the time when Caruso sang in *Don Giovanni*, the pitch of A-natural was calibrated at 441 vibrations a second (when Mozart wrote it, it was 437). Today it is 444 in many orchestras, and you can feel the difference in orchestras, whether you are singing in Berlin or Vienna or Milano. Sometimes you must sing with an orchestra three or four nights before you adjust and if you are on tour, you generally have to leave the next day to sing with a new orchestra." According to Corelli the Berlin Philharmonic, at 446, has the greatest elevation, with La Scala, in the month of December, a close contender. (Partial to the added luster of the heightened pitch, La Scala goes up to add brilliance to the orchestra's tone at the beginning of the symphony season in October, reduces the level at the opening of the opera season two months later.) The Metropolitan Opera Orchestra, which plays only for singers, maintains a steady 441—except on Saturday night, the second performance of the day, when the pitch is slightly elevated.

Onstage, shivering in the gray garret of Puccini's Bohemians, Rodolfo, falsely jovial, nervously paces from bed to stove, circling the table, attempting to join the bonhomie of his fellow artists, Marcello, Colline, and Schaunard. Anxiously repeating a vain litany of hollow gestures that includes wringing his hands, rubbing the back of his neck, stroking his chin, and hooking his thumbs into his vest pockets, he succeeds only in projecting the awkward elbows and good intentions of the high school football captain pressed against his will into the lead in the class play.

Corelli's manner toward his partners, particularly the ladies, was once a subject of some speculation. Some said that when the romantic young tenor slipped an affectionate arm around their waists, he hung on with the strength of a boa constrictor, squeezing the breath right out of them. Birgit Nilsson protested that during a performance of *Tosca,* Corelli became so agitated that he bit his nails while they were singing a love duet. Other female partners complained that, worse than nail-biting, was Corelli's ungentlemanly habit of stranding them during their solos while he walked offstage to suck moist sponges and refresh his throat.

But tonight there is no evidence of any lapse in Corelli's gallantry toward Lucine Amara's Mimì. Never taking his eyes from Mimì, he begins "Che gelida manina" on his knees (a small one-upmanship on Beniamino Gigli who courted extra applause by singing Rodolfo's narrative seated). Rising, Rodolfo seats himself on the edge of the table, his hands on his hips, one leg artfully extended, the other relaxed on a chair. With Amara's smile of encouragement to warm him, Corelli's voice grows lighter, expanding as the melody unfolds with a slow-motion grace, its strands floating gently upward, finally to dissolve in a thousand tiny points of light. When Mimì's vibrant soprano blends with Rodolfo's sweet supple tenor in "O soave fanciulla" there is no doubt among the listeners that these two artists are simpatico. They even finish together.

That has not always been the case. Callas instructed the sopranos enrolled in her master class at Juilliard, "Always save a little breath for your final note—the tenor will do the same." The legend that his fans timed him with stopwatches grew up around Corelli's virtuoso ability to hang on to high notes. At a rehearsal of one of his early *Carmens* he persisted in holding the B at the end of the flower aria which concludes the second act until the frazzled conductor threatened to dismiss him. The opera lover's favorite story of soprano-tenor battle of the lungs is, of course, the Nilsson-Corelli contretemps at an ill-fated *Turandot* given in Boston during a Metropolitan tour. When Miss Nilsson recklessly clung to the final C of the aria "In questa reggia" for several seconds after Corelli ran out of breath, the miffed tenor retired to his dressing room in a pout. Attempting to soothe Corelli, Bing advised him to take his revenge by biting Nilsson instead of kissing her during the seduction scene in the final act. Following Bing's advice, Corelli is said to have nipped Nilsson hard on the neck and after the performance the diva wired Bing, who had hastily taken an early plane back to New York: "Cannot go on to Cleveland. Have tenor rabies."

"It is a good story," Corelli nods, his brown eyes sparkling mischievously, "but it did not happen. I did not bite Miss Nilsson." He merely warned her, he claims. When Nilsson as Princess Turandot wailed, "La mia gloria è finita!" ("my glory is finished"), instead of replying in the words of the

libretto, "No, è commincita" ("No, it is just beginning"),
Corelli sang in clear round tones, "Si, è finito!"

"Every singer is born with something special. There are
people who use personality; there are some who have a
magnificent legato. Others have a marvelous *mezza voce*—
you use what you have," Corelli explains. "When I began
making my career I used the long notes because it was a
quality of my voice that interested the public. Today I
realize you see the artist not in a single glorious note or in
a beautiful phrase or an aria, but also in a recitative and
in the ensemble." Conceding that continued overexposure
in the musical upper reaches is flirting with vocal suicide,
Corelli confirms that he has grown more parsimonious toward dispensing high tones with an extra half-life. "It
makes a terrific impression, but you must not do more than
one a performance. The extra strength needed softens the
throat, and if you spend all your energy on beautiful effects
while you are young, you will be vocally bankrupt at fifty."

Nonetheless, a man's voice, maintains Corelli mirrors his
mentality in a tone painting of his interior landscape. "My
voice sounds the way I am inside," he believes. "I am a man
who likes to do dangerous things, I like adventure. I like
to do things with the voice that may be too difficult for it.
Sometimes I extend it. Not too often. Many more times I go
back to my dressing room, look in the mirror, and say,
Corelli, *stupido*, if you had taken the easy way it would be
all right. Sometimes I do not agree with the composer, I
feel another expression is more appropriate, I think eighty
percent of the time we must oblige the composer by remaining faithful to the score, but we cannot become enslaved
by tradition. Times change. What was beautiful fifty years
ago may not be considered beautiful now."

Pausing reflectively for a moment, he adds that there is

another dilemma with tradition. "The people who initiated
a style of singing an aria or a special fioritura had a natural
facility for it which succeeding generations may lack. In
*Werther,* for instance, the tenor aria "Pourquoi me réveiller"
ends in E-flat. The tradition in Italy is that the tenor who
sings *Werther* holds this note for a very long time and then
ends with a big diminuendo. For me the big diminuendo is
the most difficult thing I can ask of my voice."

The diminuendo has been a preoccupation of twenty-five
years for Corelli. He keeps returning to the "Celeste Aïda,"
the first important aria he learned and the one with which
he won both his earliest singing contest and first national
competition. Winthrop Sargeant, former *New Yorker* music
critic, has written that for him "Celeste Aïda" is the line of
demarcation between the artistry of a Caruso and a routine
tenor. The artist, asserts Sargeant, emphasizes the middle
syllables of the words *Aïda* (Ah-EE-da) and *divina* (dee-
VEE-na) in the opening phrases "Celeste Aïda, forma
divina." The hacks, on the other hand, blast the final
syllables which lie in the most powerful section of the tenor's
range. Questioning Sargeant's law, Corelli points out that
Caruso placed nearly equal stress on the second and third
syllables in both his 1906 and 1908 recordings of that aria.
Corelli, who has carefully studied recordings of this aria by
all this century's preeminent tenors, discovered an instruc-
tion in Verdi's score generally overlooked by most other
singers. For many years he was not able to achieve the
desired effect. In his own 1964 recording it is missing, but
in 1967, first on the stage at Lincoln Center, and then in a
recording of *Aïda* made with Birgit Nilsson, Corelli hit his
mark: a final B-flat concluding the aria begun at full voice,
gradually thinning to the trailing pianissimo Verdi pre-
scribed. "At first people thought I did it with special en-

gineering—but I have even more beautiful examples of that diminuendo on tapes of live performances," Corelli remarks not in the least bit boastfully.

Like many theater people, Corelli holds critics in low esteem. The evolution of a critic, according to Corelli, goes like this: "The critic goes to the theater and he writes what the public thinks, how the public reacts. Then he changes: he begins to write what he feels. Finally he ceases paying attention to any reactions by his two thousand companions in the audience. Rossini said the most important quality for an opera singer was 'Voice, voice, voice,' like a machine. But what made Caruso's voice special is that heart that nobody else has ever had. His heart was bigger than his voice, full of the sun of Napoli, but filled with *tristesse,* too. It could open your heart, that voice, it could conquer an empire, but maybe not a critic."

Of his dedication to his art there is no question. Corelli is eager to please, and his democratic philosophy is that what pleases the majority of his audience most of the time must be right. With the opera house shaking under wave after wave of applause, who can blame him if he ignores the sourpuss who protests a glorious C where an austere A-flat appears in the score.

But if he pays little attention to music journalists, Corelli is an unrelenting judge of himself. "Don't come into my dressing room if you come only for compliments," he warns. "I don't want people who hear a routine performance to rub their hands and say, 'You know, you were in good voice tonight.' I suffer. For me singing is not a mission, mission is too big a word. But I should like to do a good performance every time. Sometimes you don't feel well, your throat is not good, you have the flu, you don't sleep

Franco Corelli as Rodolfo in Puccini's *La Bohème* (*Photo by Erika Davidson*)

the night before—many things happen during the year if you do sixty or seventy performances. Big famous artists sometimes crack a note—it is human. But don't tell me I sing well when I don't." He likes to ask the little people what they think about his performance, those who have no money but go to standing room because they love opera. These are the only critics in Corelli's eyes. For his part, Corelli attends only performances by great artists, so that he can learn and because "I prefer not to hear people who will place me in the position of being critical."

A livelihood that depends on feelings and sensations spawns an eccentric strain of behavior commonly labeled temperament. Sometimes it is a signal that a career is about to begin, or that one is at ebb. Often it is an artist's petition for parole from the painful isolation and the morbid fear of failure that form the leitmotiv of his days. Certainly every great artist has temperament; none could survive without it. With each fresh outburst he affirms his need for the public's love and reestablishes his own personal identity. Flattered, the public encourages ever more colossal displays.

For all his natural artistic and personal gifts, from the beginning of his life onstage Corelli has been afflicted with deep-rooted feelings of inferiority, which in combination with his narcissism and touchy Latin pride occasionally proved a highly combustible mixture. A keen sense of melodrama, together with the faulty inner equilibrium and inconsistencies of mood associated with the creative personality, has contributed to exhibitions of artistic temperament whose high degree of visibility in mid-twentieth-century opera were chiefly rivaled by those of Maria Callas. In fact, in a revealing remark, Corelli commented that when he first met Callas in 1953, while she was well-known throughout Italy, in the rest of Europe and in her native United States, no one knew her name. "Then she began having blowups with the biggest maestri," Corelli recalled. "A year later, when I met Callas again, she was the most famous opera singer in the world."

For a time it appeared that Corelli might make a career simply of being Corelli.

*Verona.* In the first-act intermission of *Madama Butterfly* Corelli learned that the conductor had commented disparagingly on the tenor's erratic tempi. Locating the villain lounging against a wall of the stadium, Corelli hissed: "Maestro, I know I cannot punch you in the nose." With the perplexed conductor looking on, Corelli began slamming his fist into the stone. When his knuckles and fingers were battered and bleeding, he shook hands with the conductor, saying, "Maestro, you now have my blood on your conscience." Returning to the stage, he sang magnificently despite his not altogether successful efforts to prevent Butterfly from squeezing his hand during the love duet.

*Milan.* En route to La Scala, with no time to spare, to sing in a performance of *La Forza del Destino,* Corelli noticed in his rearview mirror that another car was creeping up on his silver Ferrari. He floored the accelerator; still the other car, a Jaguar, overtook him. As it sped by, in a fit of fury Corelli jammed his fist through his own car window. That night Don Alvaro appeared with one hand encased in a mit of adhesive.

*Florence.* Often he is a victim of his own urgent pursuit of perfection. Practicing the piano at home, repeatedly Corelli failed to invest a particular phrase with what he considered to be the proper intonation. Finally, unable to endure the frustration any longer, he leaped off the piano bench and smashed his fist through the closet door. Tug as they might, the joint efforts of Corelli and his wife to release the imprisoned hand were unavailing, and a carpenter had to be summoned to set free the mollified singer.

*Rome.* While rehearsing *Don Carlo* at the Rome Opera House, baritone Boris Christoff rashly attempted to upstage Corelli. The offender quickly paid for that piece of impertinence with a nightmare moment of undiluted terror as the irate tenor, seizing a nearby dagger, threatened to stab him in the hand.

*Parma.* Retribution may not be swift; nevertheless, punishment always follows the crime. In 1959 at the Teatro Regio, Maestro Romano Gandolfi committed the double error of dropping the curtain while Corelli was still singing the high C that terminates the third act of *Il Trovatore,* then subsequently asserting that in his opinion Carlo Bergonzi was a superior Manrico. Surprisingly, Corelli remained mute. But five years later, on December 7, 1963, following a triumphant opening of *Cavalleria Rusticana* at La Scala, while the hall still thundered with cheers for Turiddu, Corelli spotted Gandolfi, then a coach at Milan, backstage. In a split second Corelli had grabbed the luckless fellow by the throat. "Do you still think Bergonzi is better than me?" he raged, as the house ushers rushed to separate them.

*Naples.* By now a legend is the historic mishap which occurred involving Corelli and a member of the audience in the San Carlo opera house. Again the culprit was *Trovatore.* The popular mezzo-soprano Fedora Barbieri was singing the role of Azucena, Manrico's gypsy mother. The curtain fell to warm applause at the end of Azucena and Manrico's duet which closes the second act, and the singers returned to acknowledge the audience's appreciation. But as they were taking their bows, a sharp cry of *Barbieri sola!*

*sola!*" ("Barbieri, come out alone") rang out from a box overhead. Considering himself insulted, the incensed tenor, still dressed in his officer's coat of mail, rushed backstage, bolted three flights of stairs, and located the source of the shouting. Finding the box locked from within, he broke down the door and confronted Mario Improta, a twenty-two-year-old student. "I will wait for you outside after the show," Corelli fumed, impetuously slapping Improta's face. The two fell to scuffling noisily with Corelli pounding the Barbieri admirer's chest. Just as he was about to draw his stage sword, several members of the San Carlo staff arrived and dragged him away. For the next twenty minutes Corelli could not speak. Then, his bruised sensibilities still smarting, he went back onstage and sang a stirring exposition of "Di quella pira" ("Tremble, ye tyrants!").

"Most of the time I am very reasonable," maintains Corelli, absently rubbing the ears of the poodle who has curled up on the sofa beside him. "But I live on nerves. Opera is not singing in front of a microphone with a small voice. When I am nervous I must put out what I have inside in my stomach." His right hand closes in a fist; the third and fourth knuckles are enlarged and have each been broken more than once. "When I am with others, I try to stay within the limits of the situation (it does not matter how I punish myself when I am alone). But if there are one or two words extra," he strikes a match by way of illustration, "the temper flares up and a fight can come easily because performers are all nervous people.

"I was not angry with Boris Christoff," he continues, "he was angry with me." According to Corelli, Christoff complained about the tenor's prominent positioning onstage. When the director insisted that the rehearsal continue, with Corelli in his place, Christoff appeared to agree. The

end of the scene called for Filippo to lunge at the soldier
with his sword; Christoff assaulted Corelli with such relish
onlookers gasped, convinced the attack was real. Corelli,
of the same opinion, jumped back screaming "*Verimente,
verimente!*" When Christoff pursued, jabbing Corelli's leg
cruelly several times, "I had to defend myself," Corelli
explains. "One leg was bleeding and I saw that he knew
what he was doing."

Corelli's recollection of the Naples incident emphasizes
humor rather than violence, and as he describes it, the
resulting imbroglio could easily qualify for a Marx Brothers
scenario.

"The man was a Barbieri fan, she was his idol. At the end
of the second act he screamed at her, 'I want you alone,
come out alone.' In Italy it is the custom that we take our
bows together, never alone. And I was so sure that I sang
well that I asked him, 'What did you say?' He repeated,
'I want the mezzo alone.'"

"This was for me unjust. Now I am the first critic in the
world for myself: if other people think my performance is
50 percent good, for me it is only 10 percent satisfactory.
That night I knew I sang a beautiful second act—the role
is not so difficult that I would make a mistake. I was in the
right, so I must insist that the man apologize.

"The act was over so I went behind the curtain and
opened the door into the corridor. The patrons were filing
out of their boxes. They were in evening clothes and I was
running through them with my cape flying and my sword
clanking. In the back of me my colleagues were chasing me
yelling: 'Corelli, Corelli—what's the matter? What are you
doing? You're crazy, Corelli!' Along the way we picked up
half the chorus.

"When I arrived at the door of the box, many people got

Franco Corelli (*Photo Courtesy of Christian Steiner/Angel Records*)

out of their seats to see me. It is not usual to see the tenor of the opera in the audience. I found the door was locked and I put my shoulder to it and broke it down. The man was facing the stage, still applauding. When I touched his shoulder, he looked at me with great surprise—and fear. I was ready to punch him when the director of San Carlo arrived, shouting 'Do you want to ruin yourself?'"

The director, it seemed, was anxious to effect a speedy truce because seated in the adjacent box, conspicuous to all but the embattled tenor and Barbieri's gallant champion, was the Commissioner of Police. "If there is some action in court, I will have to report that this tenor invaded a private citizen's box," threatened the Commissioner, and fifty minutes later, when Corelli cooled down, the performance resumed. Today the Corellis and Improta, now a lawyer, and whose regard for Barbieri never faltered, are friends and have dinner whenever the Corellis return to Italy. Corelli's most vivid recollection of the whole incident is the chase: "The chorus looked so funny chasing me—they lost their wigs."

*"Are you unhappy with what you are doing, have you worries that keep you awake, is your love life unsatisfied? Don't have fear. The last word isn't yours, it all depends on a stroke of luck."*

Corelli wrote these words of consolation in a letter to a troubled friend. Luck and destiny sound a pervasive theme weaving itself in and out of his conversation and thoughts, joyous or mournful with mood and circumstance, yet in the end remaining essentially unchanged.

*"In Italy everybody sings at one time during his life. I began as a joke—nobody begins with the idea of becoming famous. I found success the easy way. I was very lucky."*

Since he suffers a peculiar brand of fatalism that denies

him pride in victory yet renders him culpable in defeat, a large measure of Corelli's anxiety proceeds from the underlying conviction that his voice is a gift and his success some sort of divine caprice.

"When you choose to be a musician your future is a question mark. In 100,000 people, maybe one will arrive—not necessarily the talented one. Talent is no guaranty of success. When I met Beniamino Gigli toward the end of his life, in 1954, a priest was with him. After the priest left, Gigli turned to me and said, 'That is my brother. He has a fabulous voice, better than mine. But he was the son intended to enter the church. Many fabulous voices in this world are disguised as priests and bricklayers. Every man has his destiny.'"

Corelli was not a child prodigy. He did not, in fact, begin to sing until he was well into his twenties. One of four children and the son of a draftsman in the local shipyards, Corelli was born August 8, 1923, in the Adriatic port town of Ancona, Italy. "Nobody in my family was musical," he acknowledges, and the only opera he heard at home was an infrequent Caruso recording on the radio. In keeping with middle-class Italian tradition, Corelli was expected to enter his father's profession and at twelve he was enrolled at a local institute for technical draftsmen.

Vain about his appearance, Corelli dressed for school in his most elegant suits, fastidiously turned out in brilliant white shirts and silk ties while his school companions preferred loose sweaters and casual slacks. His grades were good, however, and his amiable nature and precocious athletic skill neutralized any disdain his dandyism might have provoked. Outside the classroom Corelli boxed, and one year he was the winner of the Italian Junior Rowing Championship. Life was not always as open and lighthearted as it appeared on the surface, however.

Ancona had two juvenile gangs, the Archi and the Capo-
dimonte. The rivals fought nocturnal duels on the docks
along the sea, sometimes armed with chains and knives and
hurling rocks until mounted police, nightsticks flailing,
chased off the young toughs. For a while, like most young
men growing up in Ancona, Corelli belonged to one of the
gangs, the Archi, and participated in several waterfront
skirmishes.

Persuaded by his family to continue his education, Corelli
entered the University of Bologna to study naval engineer-
ing. While he was there a friend who was an amateur
singer persuaded Corelli to accompany him to Florence
where he had entered a singing competition. The young
men stayed with some friends who also loved music, although none was a professional musician. "We listened to
some Caruso records," Corelli reminisces, "the Neapolitan
songs. Some I had heard. With the others, after I had heard
them once, the next time, at almost the same moment
Caruso sang, I could repeat the phrase. I became very
excited and I had a vision that I should change my trade.
I did not have any reason to think this—it was a sixth sense."

Anticipating a bit of fun, Corelli's friends entered his
name in the auditions. "Why don't you listen to the boy who
has the big voice, they said to the maestro. And when he
consented, I screamed so strongly the judges were impressed and I won." Corelli's shoulders hunch briefly in a
baleful shrug. "And," he adds, "I only went because I
wanted to have a trip to Florence and look at the girls."
Spending every lira of the $30 prize on entertaining several
pretty young ladies, the pair wound up hitchhiking home.

Corelli had the misfortune to grow up in a town without
a single singing teacher. The local opera house, the nine-
teenth-century Teatro Delle Muse, had been bombed out
in the early years of World War II, and with its destruction

the city's musical life rapidly faded. When Corelli returned to Bologna following his Florence adventure, his friends observed that he withdrew into himself. He lost all interest in sports. At home in Ancona, lacking a car of his own, he borrowed a neighbor's truck and began to spend his spare time touring the provinces listening to opera.

"I loved singing, from that night in Florence it became my life. But my parents had their feet on the ground. They insisted I finish school before I studied music." Since he could not read music, Corelli began teaching himself by listening hour upon hour to the records of Caruso, Gigli, Lauri-Volpi, and Fleta. His parents remained adamant in their opposition to a career in music. "My father and mother thought my voice, despite its power and volume, made an ugly sound." When he did sing, often they asked him to stop.

It was precisely the encouragement any red-blooded *ragazzo* needed to drop out of college, which did not much interest him anyway, and enter the small music conservatory at Pesaro, fifty miles north of Ancona. Following the rigorous routine with a vengeance, he sang day and night and within a few months lost the upper part of his voice. Seizing upon the natural baritone qualities of his voice, he attempted to switch to the lower register. When this proved unsatisfactory, he stopped singing altogether until his throat was healed. Badly frightened by the experience, Corelli left the conservatory taking with him what would be a life-long fear of academy music and teachers. Returning to his home study method, he began building a repertory, teaching himself entire roles from records. With one of them, *Carmen*, he auditioned for the 1952 Spoleto Festival. He was successful and his performance there was a triumph that earned him invitations to sing *Carmen* in a number of

small provincial opera houses. If the repetition grew mo-
notonous, Corelli hardly dared show it—at the time it was
the only complete role he knew.

At the urging of a talent scout who heard Corelli at
Spoleto, he was asked to sing Riccardo Zandonai's *Giulietta
e Romeo* at the Rome Opera in 1953. (Zandonai was a noted
composer during Corelli's youth, and coincidentally director
of the Pesaro Liceo until his death in 1944.) Again, his
performance was highly successful, attracting wide attention, and the following year Maria Callas persuaded La
Scala to let the romantic young tenor sing Licino to her
Giulia in Luchino Visconti's lavish revival of Gasparo
Spontini's *La Vestale.*

"Callas was then a huge woman, tall and—his arms curve
in two large half-circles describing her girth—"but with a
magnificent voice. Not the fascinating personality yet. That
came later. But the voice was unearthly. She made my
career. You see, Callas wanted many things in a partner:
the voice, of course. But also the acting, the figure, the
personality. For Licino she wanted a *capitan.*"

On the night of his debut, Corelli was so nervous that
he was terrified to be in his dressing room before the performance—an apprehensiveness he has never conquered.
Dressing at home he intended to time his arrival so that he
reached the theater ten minutes before curtain time. He
failed to take into account, however, that because the opening performance of the La Scala season is broadcast on
Italian radio, the hour is set back from nine o'clock to eight
forty-five. Corelli arrived at the stage entrance at eight forty-
one, aggravating the elderly stage manager who greeted
him with the rebuke that he could not remember Caruso
ever arriving late. "I suppose you think you're better than
Caruso," he remarked sarcastically. "Maybe, someday," the

culprit replied in a voice weak with disbelief. Twenty minutes later, however, dressed in the purple tights and minitunic of a Roman warrior, Corelli moved skittishly across the cavernous stage of La Scala toward Maria Callas, matching the soaring sunburst cadenzas and filigreed trills of La Divina with some head-filling sound of his own.

From that night Corelli's career rocketed along like a space-age missile, earning him the uncomplimentary nickname "Sputnik Tenor" from envious colleagues. More serious was the epithet "Pecorelli," a combination of his surname and the Italian word for *goat* (*"pecora"*), and an invidious reference to a malady sometimes afflicting the center section of his voice producing an unpleasant sound resembling a goat's bleat.

An openhearted singer, Corelli has a subjective voice, with the fundamental source of his strength as much heart as it is art. He has never been a believer in the immutability of a score if he feels he can communicate more effectively otherwise, although his maturity has seen increasing allegiance to the written note. Perseverance can be a kind of genius in itself. But his reluctance to trust vocal coaches in the formative years, relying instead on arduous labor allied with pure instinct for musical impulse imparted indirectly from recordings, would seem to erect unnecessary obstacles in an already hazardous course.

The early results of his untutored art were uneven. The disquieting lack of rhythmic alertness, the penchant for lingering highs could well have proceeded not from technical imperfection but flawed psychology, which a persuasive personality might have enabled him to overcome sooner. From the beginning, with strong conductors his attacks were crisp, his sound better defined.

Although vocal technique is not visible like football or

ballet, what the singer does is clear to the ear. Because
Corelli is a conscientious musician, his personalized trial-
and-error vocal method eventually paid off—although at cost,
perhaps, of the painful insecurity which continues to tor-
ment him. Complimented on the beauty of a performance,
he despairs: "No, it was not good tonight. I cut one-half
beat from the first note of the aria offstage in act two."

Nevertheless, constant study and restudy of his roles
after he became a superstar enabled Corelli to improve
with each succeeding season. He pays more attention to
tempi, has perfected his timbre and acquired the patience
to fulfill each phrase instead of rushing headlong for the
glories at the top. He refined the coarse edge at the center,
excising the bleat, and his whole range has grown more
equal. Production is naturally less fluent at fifty-one than
it was at thirty; yet the years have burnished the dark baritone qualities of his voice with no impairment to its ampli-
tude and strength. Many of Corelli's contemporaries of two
decades ago—Giuseppe di Stefano and Mario Del Monaco,
for example—are at least partially retired, while his own
voice proved an unusually durable instrument and one
which retains the sensual radiance of a man in his prime.

"I know one word of German," he bewails: "*Verboten*.
It is painful for me because *Lohengrin* is one opera I have
always wanted to do. It is a favorite opera of Italian people.
Until about ten years ago in Italy we customarily sang a
few operas of foreign composers in our language and
*Lohengrin* is one of them. On my piano in Milan I have an
autographed score from Maestro Serafin that is one of my
most prized possessions. 'Before I finish my life,' he wrote,
'I should like to hear you sing *Lohengrin*.' And how I should
like to, but it would have to be in Italian, not in German."

Even for an opera singer, Corelli's linguistic infacility is pronounced. There is a shadow of a lisp, compounded by a disaffection for enunciation that can result in poorly articulated word endings. For example, an otherwise beautiful *Nessun dorma* may be marred by *o*'s which sound like *a*'s—although given the overall effect of the performance, that may be a ridiculous quibble. Learning *Werther* was particularly admirable for a singer who during the 1968 season in Florence—in an otherwise French production—felt obliged to sing the flower aria in *Carmen* in Italian. Here, too, the roots of the problem may lie in the psyche. Sniffing in the direction of the kitchen: "I'm sorry, I can hear the fish," Corelli apologizes to a visitor—a curious juxtaposition of the verbs of audition and olfaction for a musician. Later, listening to a record, he complains, "That voice doesn't look like Caruso."

Accordingly, Corelli's thirty roles, with the exception of *Carmen* and *Werther,* lie in the basic Italian repertory, with his Radames in *Aïda,* Manrico in *Il Trovatore,* and Calaf in *Turandot* the chief jewels. He likes the rigorous vocal demands of Verdi and the lyricism of Puccini, which he feels does not require a voice as richly endowed as the dramatic arias of Verdi—although in the 1973–74 Met season he turned down *Manon Lescaut* because he had never previously sung it. *Manon Lescaut,* Corelli asserts, is the greatest vocal challenge in Puccini for a man. He still enjoys an operatic challenge, but only under the proper conditions, one of which emphatically is adequate rehearsal time.

"This is what ruins opera for me today," he says. "We do too many routine performances. Performances where you go into the theater before you have had sufficient time for rehearsal. Not the kind of rehearsal where the director says, 'Okay, Desdemona, enter stage left; Iago, stand over there.' That is not a rehearsal. With forty movies available each

Franco Corelli as Calaf in Puccini's *Turandot* (*Photo by Erika Davidson*)

week on television—yes, much of it is poor, but audiences are sophisticated, they know good acting from bad. An audience cannot really know Iago unless they can read in his face what he is thinking inside."

The importance of a talented stage director in the success of opera is all too often overlooked, he feels. "The performance is born in the director's mind and he brings it to life on the stage. When I worked for the first time with Luchino Visconti at my debut at La Scala, we spent twenty-seven days in rehearsal. I was very young and very inexpert and Visconti really created me. He discovered in me a personality I didn't know I had."

For Corelli, adaptability is a director's most important quality "Ten years ago in Italy," he recalls, "we had a beautiful production of Shakespeare's *Otello* with Vittorio Gassman and Sandor Rondoni. One night Gassman would play Otello and Rondoni, Iago. The next night they reversed roles. Each interpretation was valid although they were dissimilar. One would not expect the same performance from Olivier, Gassman, Rondoni, and Richard Burton. All too often the directors we have in opera, however, want every Rodolfo to use the same gestures as his predecessor. They fail to take into account individual abilities."

"It is a mystery that the soil of Italy no longer produces the glorious voices it did forty or fifty years ago. That was a golden age abounding with great maestros and singers who lived only for singing. For seven, eight, nine years they would study. Today after one year we want to go on the stage. Today we go to the moon." Like many of his colleagues, Corelli is concerned about what lies ahead for opera. "When my parents were young," he says, "Italy was full of theaters. After all, it was the birthplace of lyric opera. When La Scala toured to Bologna or to Torino it was an event that was sold out five or six months in advance. Today they don't always fill the theater. Where once there stood one hundred opera houses, only ten remain. It is the same all over the world."

Laying the blame for the sad predicament of opera at the feet of the artists, he continues: "No longer will people come into the theater for those singers who have only one beautiful high C. The audience is not looking for a note to remember, they are looking for a night to remember—a performance that is a totally developed work of art."

While no single artist should be expected to carry the entire responsibility for the level of an individual production, Corelli charges that all too often that is the case. Stringent budgets prevent assembling casts in which all the principals are major artists, capable of giving performances of the caliber of excellence he feels is demanded by today's knowledgeable audience. "In Germany, for example, where they have a state theater, they do important productions with brilliant casts in which each singer contributes to performances with a consistently high artistic level, and every night they are sold out. At the Met, because we do not have the money, we rely on one star to compensate for many mediocre voices. We cannot have the best directors, Luchino Visconti and Franco Zeffirelli, because maybe they cost $20,000. We cannot afford Herbert von Karajan, and today von Karajan is the greatest living operatic conductor."

Momentarily sidetracked, Corelli reminisces. "You know von Karajan is an Austrian and some people will tell you Germanic people are cold. But that is not true of von Karajan. When I sing with him, he gives me the feeling that he respects me, that he likes me. He makes me feel free. With von Karajan you work hard, and you sing your most beautiful performance.

"In my mind there is one thought: What can we do to insure the future of the lyric opera?" A year ago Corelli made a complete film version of *Andrea Chénier* for Italian-German television. Somewhat skeptical at first, he emerged from the experience with the firm conviction that, skillfully used, television can be a useful tool in enlarging opera's audience. Opera is not a musical relic more appropriately consigned to a place of honor in scholarly archives: it must consider the demands of the new generation. "One generation does not look like another, you can see people change. One thing I believe most firmly is that in order to capture the attention of a newer, more youthful operagoer, we must do opera for television. But it must be properly edited so that it looks exactly like a movie." A singer in front of a camera with his mouth agape for five minutes depletes the beauty of both music and drama, he emphasizes, and not all operas would be appropriate. But *Otello, Roméo et Juliette,* and *La Bohème* are operas that, in Corelli's opinion, could be produced for television with all the force and impact of high drama.

The claims of his music are primary. Corelli's art is one of constant toil and striving for perfection. Offstage, life is hardly picturesque; he leads a sober existence, surrendering himself to his art. Yet he never seems to become bored. He thinks only of his singing and those around him must conform. Consequently, like many in his profession, he has few friends.

The center of his life is his wife, Loretta (the *e* is long, pronounced to rhyme with *we*), who has focused the full force of her considerable energies on her husband's career. Corelli's success is very much the product of a shared dream. Loretta Corelli negotiates her husband's contracts, handles his publicity, copes with his fans, acts as his manager—and prays for him right before he sings a golden C. A small redhead with crackling blue eyes and an elfin-light step, Loretta fusses over Corelli, soothes his fears, agrees that, yes, he must see the doctor for the third time in a week about his queasy stomach, smiles tolerantly behind her husband's back when he complains of feeling weak. Two minutes later Corelli, eavesdropping on Loretta's rapid-fire telephone quarrel with an Italian friend over the merits of a concert the previous evening, chortles gleefully. In the way of many other middle-aged childless couples, the Corellis indulge each other like children.

Loretta di Lelio met Corelli in 1956 in Rome when she went backstage to ask for his autograph after a performance. Although she herself had no musical ambitions, she is well suited to the life. Her father was a basso, although he died when she was very young and she never heard him perform. But she has memories of a household whose days revolved around music. She insists on remaining in the background, politely but firmly refuses to meet most reporters who come to interview her husband—"Franco is the story, I am just family."

Her presence is felt, however, watching television in another room, but with an ear cocked to be ready to jump to answer the telephone, translate a word for her husband, or insinuate herself protectively between him and a fan or journalist's naughty questions. Corelli is utterly dependent on Loretta—"Without her I can do nothing," he assures visitors who have no reason to doubt him. Joseph Conrad wrote gratefully of his wife as the person responsible for "the even flow of daily life made easy and noiseless by a tireless, silent watchful affection." It is a description that would as easily fit Loretta Corelli.

Toward late afternoon the living room of the Corelli's

West 57th Street apartment is nearly dark except for the blue glow of the television set. The furnishings are a tasteful mixture of contemporary paintings and English antiques, punctuated by occasional Oriental touches: a handsome black and gold lacquer Chinese cabinet and a porcelain vase holding a bouquet of pastel jade dogwood blossoms. In one corner is a small Steinway grand piano in a light highly polished wood, which, together with the pale green, gold, and eggshell velvets that comprise the room's predominant colors and texture, give it an airy Mediterranean look.

Corelli sits on a green velvet sofa before a low black marble table. He is informally but expensively dressed in a white cashmere shirt, gray Glen plaid slacks, and black shoes of thin glove leather. The sound is off, but the television picture is on so that he can see the stock market quotations as he listens to records—mainly Caruso, Gigli, or his old friend and mentor, Giacomo Lauri-Volpi. Since the middle fifties, Corelli has consulted with Lauri-Volpi for several weeks each summer, discussing vocal technique and characterization of the roles he is working on. Lauri-Volpi is the only "teacher" Corelli trusts, just as he has faith only in antique recordings.

"Records today don't reflect voices for what they are. Many times I hear the voice of a colleague in the theater and when I hear it on a record, I don't recognize it," Corelli confirms. "It is not the same, it is a machine voice. The engineer can make the voice larger or smaller, although he cannot give you sweetness." His own records, he says, never sound the same because the voice changes with the studio, the recording equipment, the engineer. "A singer can tell the difference between a Decca record and those of RCA or Angel," Corelli insists, "because each has a different sound." If you really want to know your voice, he adds, you must use a tape recorder which conceals nothing.

At night he will meet Maria Callas and Giuseppe di Stefano—her singing partner for the 1973–74 international tour that ended Callas's nine year self-imposed exile from the stage—for dinner at Quo Vadis. Di Stefano once threatened to cancel a concert he was giving in Philadelphia when he discovered the programs contained an advertisement for an album by "the world's greatest opera singer, Franco Corelli." (When the programs were collected and stacked in his dressing room, he consented to sing.) But the incident is long since forgotten and that is not the reason Corelli does not look forward to the evening. "I don't like to go to big places; when we are in Italy I prefer the *cantina,* the little cafes of the people." For Callas, moreover, he will put on a dinner jacket because he understands she likes to dine in elegant restaurants. Callas will understand that Loretta Corelli attended the gala Callas-di Stefano Carnegie Hall recital alone because her husband would have been in an agony of nerves for his old friend. When a mutual friend calls to report on one of the diva's earlier concerts, however, before he asks what she sang, Corelli wants to know what Callas wore and how she looked. "A little sad?" he repeats, his face falling. "Ah, but gorgeous, yes," he agrees happily, "Callas is a beautiful woman."

Despite a weakness for sports cars—at times he has owned five simultaneously—Corelli lives well but conservatively for a wealthy man. In addition to his New York residence, he owns the apartment house in Ancona where he was born, which he maintains as a home and a source of income for his elderly widowed father. He and his wife have a rambling nine-room apartment in Milan, whose signal charm, according to the proud owner, is a room installed some years ago that as nearly as possible duplicates the electronic equipment of a first-rate recording studio—all the better to study the voice. For vacations Corelli likes to go off-season to the mountain resort of Cortina d'Ampezzo in the Italian Alps where he stays in a nearly deserted hotel owned by a friend. How does he spend his holiday? Well, he plays tennis, swims, rides chair lifts to the top of the mountain where the clear air is beneficial for his throat—and he studies his roles for the coming season.

"Sometimes I ask myself, what do I care for? To refine the qualities I have in my voice—I don't know my voice, I have never heard it. For money? For glory? The glory doesn't exist. What is a moment of applause—a moment of happiness, maybe, because you can hold a note for ten seconds. If you can hold it for twenty seconds you can have as much applause as anybody can stand. For forty-five years Beniamino Gigli sang and what remains of Beniamino Gigli —nothing. The theater was never empty when Gigli was singing, and what did the Italians do when Beniamino Gigli died? They prepared a respectful commemoration. What did they want, a Caruso? Why does the voice of Caruso exist on records today; *amor d'arte?* No. Because it's big money for RCA. There is no more *amor d'arte.*"

It is difficult to recognize in the melancholy words and air of resignation the volatile spirit whose eruptions of a decade ago have permanently enlivened operatic lore. The thin wedge of fear that signals a man's early perceptions of mortality has momentarily conquered him. Then, brightening, "I heard Tito Schipa sing a concert when he was seventy-four years old, and he had a beautiful night and gave the audience much pleasure. If your body is strong, your heart is good, your voice is healthy, if you are modest, you can go on for a long time. Those who begin their careers very late," he notes with a little boy's smile, "seem to last longer."

It is the word *modest* that contains the key to Corelli: a sensitive man, rather timid, the temporary victim of his own cosmic success. The portrait that emerges is one of a gifted and dedicated artist whose shining achievement lies in serving music with his whole spirit.

# Placido Domingo

BY

*Alan Rich*

Most of the great romantic tenor roles in opera reflect some degree of instability, and the range runs from murder through philandering to puttin' on airs. The necessity to impersonate these less-than-admirable characters in the opera house may explain the equally colorful, if irrational, behavior shown by a number of tenors offstage as well. The tenor who observes these classic behavior patterns does, to be sure, make colorful copy.

Not long before sitting down to write about Placido Domingo, however, this writer had lunch with Schuyler Chapin, the Metropolitan Opera's general manager. Chapin had just come through one of the great artistic crises in the Met's recent history. The season's first performance of *Tristan und Isolde* had somehow gone on brilliantly, after 1) the scheduled Isolde (Catarina Ligendza) had canceled,

2) Jon Vickers, after arriving late for the scheduled rehearsals, withdrew from the production pleading lack of
rehearsal time, and 3) Erich Leinsdorf was pulled back from
the brink of following suit, only by the most eloquent pleading by the Met management. Chapin, when we met, was
still boiling about Vickers's tantrums, and I said to him,
"Well, at least it drew attention to the fact that Wagner's
music-drama includes a tenor role as well as a Nilsson role."
"Yes," said Chapin, "Jon really got some publicity this time."
Then conversation turned to the notion of a chapter on
Domingo in this book. "How *can* you?" Chapin asked. "He's
such a nice guy!"

Frankly, that *is* a problem. In both his personal and professional life, Domingo does somewhat break the mold. It
is difficult to find a single Domingo colleague who will not,
somewhere along the line and of his own free will, employ
the phrase "nice guy." On the stage, in those roles which he
sings as well, or better, than any other tenor in the business
today, Domingo is a small mountain of temperament, passion, a mirror of all the dramatic instabilities built into the
music created for him. Somehow, however, he has been more
successful than virtually all his colleagues in learning how to
shed his musical temperament along with his costume. This
reason alone, although there are others, is probably responsible for the fact that Domingo is almost universally admired
by even the most demanding critics in the United States and
abroad. If his work as an artist has a single flaw, it is his
failure—at least at this writing—to stir up controversy.
Research into the major critical writings in the world press,
in the decade or so that Domingo's international career has
been aloft, has failed to turn up a single important negative
review.

Among hard-core opera-lovers, whose partisanship toward

or against tenors is known for its incendiary nature, much
the same holds true. At the time Domingo made his Metropolitan Opera debut in the fall of 1968, substituting on
thirty-five minutes' notice for Franco Corelli in the role
of Maurizio in *Adriana Lecouvreur,* that house was riven
in the traditional battle areas—standing room downstairs and
the family circle (top balcony)—between the *Corellisti*
and the supporters of Carlo Bergonzi. It was possible, on
any night when either tenor was scheduled, to serve as
embarrassed witness to fits of screaming and arm-waving
in the Met's various lobbies out into the Lincoln Center
Plaza, and down into the steamy subterranean atmosphere
of the Footlights Cafeteria. Corelli's groupies had, as usual,
taken their places for the expected send-up in *Adriana*
when word circulated that Domingo was stepping in. Immediately the news went out, in that vaporous way that
rumors move around the Met's corridors, that the hapless
substitute would be in for a bad time that night. And there
was, indeed, some stirring, with a few boos mixed in, when
Domingo made his entrance. But, in a scene reminiscent
of Orpheus taming the Furies, the planned demonstration
almost immediately fell apart. Domingo, walking unarmed
onto the field, had won the fray. Since that time he has
failed utterly to stir up the hostile faction that many of
his colleagues regard as the sine qua non of a successful
career.

At thirty-three, Domingo must be described either as a
singer whose career is still on the rise, or as the youngest
fully-arrived tenor in the upper echelons. (Many of his
most ardent admirers will argue for the latter evaluation,
although he leans toward the former.) Physically, he is of
a type generally described as "burly," although the further
description of "teddy bear" has also often been used. At

six feet two, weighing in at approximately 225 pounds, he makes for a rather imposing teddy bear, although a slight corporation around the middle (which, after an old hernia acted up early in the 1973–74 season, he has vowed to get rid of) does add to this impression. So does an irresistibly boyish countenance, underpinned with just the suggestion of one chin too many. Crowning this glory is a thick mop of jet-black, wavy hair, with a thread of gray here and there that can be forgiven in anyone trying to make a career in opera these days.

Given this formidable physique, Domingo does tend to dominate any stage on which he is placed. This domination can easily be mistaken for acting, although Domingo doesn't quite do that. What he does in a role, however, may be even rarer than actual acting: he moves with total awareness of what he looks like, where he wants to go, and how he plans to get there. He does not need to push his notes beyond the footlights with a semaphoric straightening of the right arm, nor to underline the heartfelt quality of a turn of phrase with a clutch at his capacious chest. His stage movements are, in other words, remarkably graceful for a man of his size and weight.

What can also be said about Domingo's in-person presence is that—and this, too, is a rare feat among operatic singers in any vocal range—he looks the way he sounds. Taken purely as raw material, his voice is uncommonly full and vibrant. It darkens, evenly and virtually imperceptibly, from the middle G on downward, leading one to suspect—rightly as it happens—that he had once worked his way up from a light baritone. From the G on up, the timbre is remarkably rich and unvaried, free at the top of the slight reediness that Pavarotti, to name one example, has had to learn (and very successfully) to control. He has the high C but has found that it doesn't always work for him, and he prefers to take his "Di quella pira" transposed a half step down.

Given raw material of this high quality, Domingo has applied his own superior musical insights to forge a repertory of considerable breadth. Given the size of his instrument, and of the physique from which it emanates, he tends to find his finest moments in roles of a heroic stamp: Manrico, for example, or Radames or Alvaro in *La Forza del Destino*. With *Rigoletto*'s Duke he is somewhat less happy; the quiet, high-lying lyricism in the duet with Gilda and the "Parmi veder le lagrime" do challenge his usually immaculate breath control. On the other hand, he has accomplished a breath-stopping light delicacy in the few performances he has sung as Riccardo in *Un Ballo in Maschera*. It's the old story: a Rolls-Royce may stun you with its power on the open highway, but it also feels wonderful poking along in city traffic.

His range of sympathy, therefore, extends over most of the lyric repertory and all of the dramatic. Probably the most remarkable aspect of his singing is its absolute freedom. Only in the most lurid moments in late romantic opera —Canio's final scenes in *I Pagliacci*, for example, a role he doesn't much care for—does one sense that old-fashioned, melodramatic hardening of the voice, a clamping down on the tones for dramatic effect. When talking about his favorite tenors of the past—as we'll see in more detail later in this report—he does tend to reserve his greatest admiration for the open-throated, devil-may-care kind of singer (Gigli, di Stefano in his prime, Galliano Masini) over the more hard-bitten, explosive if dazzling sound of a Martinelli.

Of all the singers whom Domingo has recently worked with, the American baritone Sherrill Milnes is probably the best qualified to add his own testimonial to these words.

Placido Domingo as Cavaradossi in Puccini's *Tosca* (*Photo by Louis Mélançon*)

Domingo and Milnes have, in fact, come to be regarded as something of a "team," a fact which hasn't escaped the attention of record, as well as operatic, producers. RCA has paired them in a number of complete opera recordings and single disks of operatic duets, but the most intriguing release of all appeared in the fall of 1973: a record in which each singer had one side of famous solo arias, *conducted by the other.*

Milnes talked with me about Domingo's singing. "The most important thing about Placido," he said, "is that his timbre has *sincerity.* That sounds a little corny, I know, but it isn't, really. The hardest thing for any singer to do, actually, is to make you believe that *he* believes what he's singing. Placido has this ability; he has that vibrance in the way he makes a sound, so that you can sense the dramatic situation whether you know the words or not. Leonard Warren had that quality, and so did a few others. But not many. When Placido works *on* a role, he really works *in* the role, and when he's on top of it, he makes it alive. Not by acting; no, he does something a lot harder: he makes the role live simply by its sound."

We talked a little about the so-called "team." "Placido and I work well together," Milnes went on, "mostly because we can discuss problems together. With other tenors, when there is a problem in a duet involving, say, where to breathe, we have to go to the conductor and let him make the final decision. But with Placido I know that he and I can work out these problems together. He has this incredible intelligence about music. It's not just an instinct; he really *knows,* knows what he's doing, knows why, knows the music. When he has a problem, or when we have one together, we take it over to the piano, and Placido sits and plays and the problem gets solved. He doesn't just play like a tenor; he really plays that goddamn piano."

Milnes and Domingo, in fact, also have in common the ability to perform music other ways than by singing, which is what led to the recording of their joint debuts as conductors. "That might strike you as some sort of gimmick," Milnes said. "But it wasn't. Placido and I had both studied conducting in our early days. My mother had an oratorio society in my hometown, Downers Grove, Illinois, and I used to prepare the orchestra for her concerts. Since she died, four years ago, I've gone home to conduct at least one concert a year for them.

"Anyhow, that record gave us a chance to expand our work as a 'team,' and we both worked hard at it. After all, we had the New Philharmonia Orchestra to deal with, not just some pick-up group. Each of us discussed phrasing with the other, and we played beautifully to each other's strengths. Weaknesses, too. Take one of Placido's arias, the 'Parmi veder' from *Rigoletto*. He's not very comfortable in that opera, as you know, and especially feels that that aria is not for him. That very high, light, opening phrase is a killer for anyone with that big a voice. So here's what we decided upon. I conducted that last descending line, those repeated chords before the aria, with a rather big crescendo. That gave Placido the chance to start out on something like a mezzoforte, which he then shaded down by a diminuendo. It's a trick, I know, but it's the sort of thing that can happen when two people who really respect each other work together. And it certainly got him into the aria neatly.

"Sure, Placido is a fighter. He's a nice guy, but don't let that fool you. He competes all over the place, but only when it's honest. He won't upstage you; he won't take unfair advantage, like—you name him, I won't. But if he thinks you're not cutting the music, he'll sing you under the table. And believe me, he can."

The notion of discussing any singer of opera in terms of musicianship, or musical sensitivity, is lost on a certain percentage of the nightly audience that has come to regard the vocal side of opera as a kind of high-class circus act done without tightropes but aimed at the same nerve centers that are touched by dazzling feats on the high wire. Sensitivity, to such people, is one of those things, like freckles, that may be amusing to contemplate but quite beside the point. Given the raw vocal material of a Placido Domingo, the additional fact of his musical awareness and reactive powers is even more beside the point. Yet, these qualities are built-in elements of Domingo's personality, and if he regards them as unnecessary encumbrances, he has been successful so far in keeping that fact a secret. Their presence may be partially explained—if, indeed, explanation is necessary—by certain facts in his artistic upbringing.

Domingo was born, on January 21, 1941, in Madrid, the political but far from the artistic capital of Spain. Madrid's history as a cultural center has always been, to say the least, spotty. It has a scratchy, mediocre symphony orchestra, supports a few chamber ensembles, is visited now and then by opera troupes from elsewhere in Europe, but shows little need to support any opera of its own. (A few years ago the beginnings of a publicly raised fund for an opera house was diverted by the government toward a superhighway from Madrid to Barcelona.) The one art form that is supported with any degree of fervor by the Madrileños is the zarzuela, the popular operetta that typically uses a pastiche of composed and folk tunes, usually short and frivolous. Placido's parents, Placido Domingo, Sr., and Pepita Embil, were the stars of a successful zarzuela company; Pepita, in fact, is still widely known as the "Queen of the Zarzuela." In 1949 the elder Domingos toured with a troupe

to Latin America, where they again found delighted
audiences. The rest of the troupe returned to Spain following the tour; the Domingos, however, remained in Mexico
City and founded a company of their own which is still
flourishing. Young Placido's first musical experiences were
centered around his parents' activity. He had shown, from
an early age, a good musical ear and an agreeable voice,
and almost from the beginning of the Mexican venture he
was allowed on the stage in bit parts. (Apparently, no
zarzuela can expect much of a run without a part for a
small boy somewhere, and a still younger Domingo, Placido's son by his first marriage, has now also sung with his
father and grandparents in Mexico City.)

By his early teens, young Placido had continued to demonstrate a growing musical talent, which his parents gladly
encouraged. He began formal studies in piano, privately,
and at fourteen entered the Mexico City Conservatory.
While there, he continued to spend his spare hours with his
parents' troupe, singing until his voice broke, playing the
piano at rehearsals, once in a while even conducting.

Singing, however, was still far from his thoughts—at least
as a full-time prospect. His early work at the Conservatory
was mostly involved with musical basics: more piano,
harmony, and theoretical studies. At sixteen he was briefly
married, about which he now says little except that it
forced him to drop his studies and find work. He cast
around the city, picking up some money as an accompanist,
a little more as pianist for the local Metropolitan Opera
auditions, and still more playing in nightclubs. In the course
of the latter work, he puts it quite simply, "I found out
I could sing."

His marriage ended by divorce, Domingo returned to the
Conservatory, now with the notion of becoming a singer

further forward in his plans. He audited all the vocal classes the school offered, "just to hear all the singers, what they could do, their various techniques." One of these classes was taught by Carlo Morelli, an Italian baritone who had had a middling career in Europe and the United States in the 1920s, and who had retired to Mexico City to teach. Morelli, as the Conservatory's ranking vocal authority, taught interpretation to advanced singers rather than the nitty-gritty of technique, but he was apparently impressed with the tall young man who sat in on his classes.

"I auditioned for Morelli as a baritone," Domingo recalls. "In fact, I had the gall to come in with the Prologue from *Pagliacci*. The first thing he did was to inform me that I was a tenor. 'You can give me the Lion (Leon) in Leon-cavallo, but not the Horse (Cavallo).'

"Morelli was a fantastic man. Even at his age, he had a fantastic range, all the baritone quality and all the way up to the top of the tenor register. He could go up to the B-flat in 'Come un bel dì di maggio,' the big tenor show-piece in *Andrea Chénier*, without even realizing it.

"But we almost never talked about singing. We talked, instead, about *meaning:* what the words mean, what the musical line means. That was all he cared about. I never knew, with him, when my way of singing a certain line changed from my own dull way to the way he wanted it. The change simply occurred. We'd take an aria. He would sing it first, explaining to me the weight, the meaning of each word. Then I would try to do the same thing, and we would talk about it. No, I don't mean I would try to *do* the same thing; it's more that I would try to *feel* the same thing, to find out what Morelli had been thinking when he sang the aria. The most important thing Morelli taught me, beyond anything about singing or interpretation of one aria or another, was how to think. He would say, over and over, that thinking was the greatest gift a singer could have."

Morelli died in 1971, late enough to see his pupil's own thinking pay off. Domingo wears a ring given to him by Morelli's widow after his death.

During his time with Morelli, at about seventeen or eighteen, Domingo met another young singer, Marta Ornelas, whose career in Mexico City had already been launched. She, too, was a thinking singer, a specialist in German lieder, and the codirector of a small touring group that performed chamber opera and similar specialized fare. Domingo and Marta fell in love, kept company for three years, and, in 1962, were married. During part of their courtship years Domingo served as pianist for her small opera company.

But meanwhile, Domingo continued to work slowly at his vocal career. In 1958 a touring company of *My Fair Lady* came to Mexico, with Spanish-singing leads, and with smaller roles to be cast from local singers. Domingo auditioned for the company and pulled down a small role, one of the drunken companions of Alfred P. Doolittle. He also understudied the role of Freddie, and sang it on the stage a few times during the 200-performance run of the show. That was his first professional experience, the first time he had earned a role by auditioning for it. From here there was no turning back.

"Several people in the cast told me, during the run of the show, that I should be singing opera. But I still was unsure whether they were right or not. Naturally, since I was working, I didn't have the chance to hear very much opera myself in those days. But I did listen to records quite a bit, trying to 'absorb' the singing of others. Who? Caruso,

Placido Domingo with his family (*top to bottom, left to right*): Jose, Placido, Jr., Alvaro and Marta (*Photo by Erika Davidson*)

in particular, and also, very much, Giuseppe di Stefano. Di Stefano was the first tenor I ever heard in person, in *Tosca* in 1959."

What made decisions even more difficult was that Domingo was still pursuing other lines of musical endeavor, along with singing. The great Franco-Russian conductor Igor Markevitch was then also teaching at the Conservatory. Markevitch, in addition to his own gifts as a conductor, was until his death the most sought-after teacher of conducting anywhere in the world. His classes in Florence and, later, in Mexico turned out a healthy percentage of the under-forty conductors active in the world today. With Markevitch, Domingo could build on the rudimentary experience he had already gleaned in his parents' theater; elsewhere at the Conservatory, he continued to develop his techniques and insights as a pianist. Thus, the decision as to which road to follow was complicated by the availability of enticing alternatives.

But the lure of the voice rang out over the alternatives, and in 1959 Domingo presented himself for audition at Mexico City's opera house. This was a company with an illustrious tradition; next to Argentina's Colón it was and still is considered the finest of Latin American houses. Its management also has a fine reputation for its ability to spot important talent at an early stage. Mexico's opera house, for example, is where Maria Callas sang her first professional opera in the Western Hemisphere, and the pirated recordings from her Mexico days are eagerly handed around by that singer's admirers.

Marta was then also singing major roles at the house, which surely spurred Domingo's decision to audition there. "Once again, however, I started by making the same mistake I had made for Morelli. I started my audition with a group

of baritone arias, only to be told I was a tenor. And so I
switched. I cracked, or croaked, or did *something* awful on
'Amor ti vieta,' but I got a contract anyhow. My debut was
as Borsa in *Rigoletto,* and that was followed by the Abbé
in *Dialogues des Carmélites:* nothing very big, you see, but
at least I was in."

Upon landing the contract, Domingo immediately returned to Morelli for further coaching, and also began what
little formal training he ever received as an actor, some
classes in 1960 with the television director Seki Sano. This
immediately began to lead in yet another direction; during
the 1961–62 season Domingo directed a series of dramatic
programs for Mexico City television, and also appeared
with the group in small dramatic roles.

But opera still cast its spell, and the next few years in
Domingo's career fall into the traditional mold, the story
of a bright young singer gradually working his way up from
one-line parts to two-line parts and, eventually, to leads. In
1960 he took on some more musical comedy work (*Redhead,*
*Brigadoon*), along with some work at the small opera
house in Monterrey—which is related to the Mexico City
house the way a farm club might be related to a big-league
baseball team. At Monterrey he took on a couple of *com-
primario* parts: Remendado in *Carmen,* Ping ("or was it
Pang?—I don't remember") in *Turandot,* and the more
substantial role of Cassio in *Otello.* Then came the first big
break, Alfredo in *La Traviata,* in Monterrey. ("On May
19 . . . I'll never forget that date. In the last act I literally
broke into tears. I thought I'd never be able to finish.")
Also, in 1961, he had his first chance to sing a major role
with Marta, in a romantic opera called *Ultimo Sueño* by a
minor Mexican composer named Vázquez. ("It's a verismo
piece, about a man who brings his dead wife back to life.")

Later in 1961, back in Mexico City, Domingo served ringing notice of his presence with a Cavaradossi in *Tosca*. That
proved an important night, because it provided the key that
opened the road beyond the border. Nicola Rescigno, music
director of the Dallas Civic Opera, was conducting in
Mexico City that season and had his ears open. He heard
Domingo and brought him to Dallas, where he sang the
hapless Arturo in a *Lucia di Lammermoor* that starred Joan
Sutherland. For the next year Domingo did a considerable
amount of commuting across the Mexican border: a Pinker-
ton in a Tampa *Butterfly*, another Arturo in New Orleans,
and an Edgardo to Lily Pons's Lucia in Fort Worth, that
lady's last appearance on an operatic stage.

By now it was 1962, and both members of the Domingo
household were actively pondering their operatic futures.
Word reached them that the Hebrew National Opera in
Tel Aviv was looking for a leading soprano and tenor. Ap-
plication was made and accepted.

The Domingos remained in Tel Aviv for two and one-half
years, he singing in 280 performances, she in 150: the best
possible seasoning for a couple still barely into their
twenties. "This was where I *really* began to learn how to
sing, for the first time in my life. It was like being reborn.
I was able to find out all the things I was doing wrong, in
breathing for example. Morelli had taught me how to think
about music, and he taught me how to create a character.
But nobody had ever taught me how to breathe properly
—the sort of thing that a European or an American singer
learns first of all." Marta worked on his vocal problems with
him, and he on hers. The most important thing is that he
was singing major repertory—*Faust, Carmen, Eugene
Onegin, Bohème, Don Giovanni* (with Marta as Elvira)—in
a reputable house, but one that was at the same time out

of the international mainstream, out of the constant scrutiny of the big-time critics and impresarios.

The Domingos packed up again in the spring of 1965 and headed back for Mexico, but via a stop in New York that proved to be a crucial milestone in both careers. They had, by this time, a one-year-old son, Placido III, whose demands had pretty well convinced Marta that from then on *her* career would be her family. Placido, however, put his New York visit to solid professional use. He auditioned for the Washington Opera for the 1965–66 season, and pulled down an assignment as Don José in *Carmen*. He auditioned for the lively and reputable summer season at Chautauqua, New York, and was engaged as Samson for that summer. Most importantly, he was heard by Julius Rudel of the New York City Opera Company, and was engaged, again for Don José, for the 1965 fall season.

The City Opera was then in its last months at its old quarters at the New York City Center on West Fifty-fifth Street, where it had made its shaky but promising start twenty-two years previously. It was still, as it had always been up to then, a company that welcomed young talent, trained them in its own brand of lively, enterprising, make-do opera-as-theater, and paid them peanuts. The company was admired for its ensemble, although the critics did note the presence of a number of above-average singers in the group who might someday bear watching: Beverly Sills, Norman Treigle, and another promising young tenor named Michele Molese. But cast changes at the City Opera were so frequent, and often so frantically underrehearsed, that it was impossible for the working press of New York to keep track of all the new talent that moved on and off its creaky stage. Domingo sang two *Carmen* performances that fall, and also stepped into one *Madama Butterfly* on short notice. If he was noticed at all in New York that season, the notice was barely passing; the City Opera press office was unable to produce a single mention of Domingo in the major press of the city from that first season.

But Julius Rudel did notice him, which is what really mattered in the long run. The company was about to move to luxurious new quarters at Lincoln Center's New York State Theater, and it was planning to initiate this move with a splash: a season with several premieres of new works, and the beginning of a wholesale overhaul of its standard repertory, to be restaged on new sets fitting their surroundings. The company, in other words, had decided to strike out for the big time. Opening night at the State Theater, February 22, 1966, was to be the premiere of an opera by Alberto Ginastera, one of the most respected composers in the Americas, a man whose craggy, challenging

Placido Domingo as Manrico in Verdi's *Il Trovatore* (*Photo Courtesy of RCA Records*)

instrumental works were making their way into the
repertories of adventurous soloists and orchestras throughout the world. For the City Opera's housewarming,
Ginastera provided *Don Rodrigo,* a powerful, vivid, enormously demanding work that required, among other things,
clusters of brass instruments placed out in the auditorium,
echoing each other and engulfing the audience in massive,
brutal sounds, Rudel wanted a work that would have been
clearly impossible to produce in the old quarters, and he
got one.

Domingo was given the title role, the choice being aided
by his imposing stature, the command of easy volumes of
sound that he had worked so hard, and so successfully,
to acquire during his stay in Tel Aviv—plus the not inconsiderable advantage of his native ability to sing in
Spanish. *Don Rodrigo* was a huge success—for Ginastera,
for the company, not quite for the hall (where the acoustics
were found slightly wanting), but for Rudel's courage, and
for Domingo. His appearance was taken as a debut, and
this time the press noted him well. Everyone was happy,
that is, except Domingo himself. He didn't like the music,
didn't like to sing it, and plans never to do so again.

"I didn't even see the score until after the contract was
signed, and when I saw it I was horrified. I had never sung
that kind of music before, all those atonal intervals where
you get no support at all from the orchestra, and have to
support yourself from within. That kind of singing can
really break your voice." Thus, during that whole triumphant
spring of 1966, while *Don Rodrigo* became the hottest
ticket-item in town and the crowd accorded Domingo standing ovations at every performance, he sat and fumed. The
press touted him as a great specialist in modern music.
Sarah Caldwell, of the Opera Company of Boston, offered

him the part of Aaron in the premiere she was planning of
Schoenberg's craggy *Moses and Aaron.* Domingo took one
look at the score and laughed.

But he was also shrewd enough to stay put at the City
Opera, somewhat mollified by the news that the company's
plans for him included a wide slice of the romantic repertory, most of it in newly staged productions. The
atmosphere backstage attracted him greatly and appealed
to his musical conscience and intelligence. City Opera life,
despite the move to elegant quarters, remained challenging
and unstructured. In the fall of '66, Frank Corsaro created
a brilliant new *Traviata,* with the marvelously appealing
and ingenious Patricia Brooks as Violetta and Domingo as
Alfredo. It still remains one of the best, most inventive
stagings of a traditional opera in any company's repertory.
"We all admired what Frank was doing, and so we all
worked just a little bit harder to bring it off. After rehearsals I'd go home with Frank and we'd sometimes sit
until 3 A.M., just discussing the production and planning
little things for me to do. That kind of closeness is not
very common in a large opera house, and I still remember
those City Opera days for that reason." Among the "little
things" that Domingo and Corsaro worked out was one
stunning effect that you had to have seen to realize its
poignancy. Alfredo rushes into the dying Violetta's room
in the last act; she totters toward him and falls into his
arms, whereupon he picks her up and carries her to the
window as they begin the "Parigi, o cara" duet. He holds
her in his arms for the entire duet. Not many tenors have
the lung power to carry off that kind of feat, and it certainly
isn't recommended for performances in which, say, Enrico
di Giuseppe is singing with, say, Montserrat Caballé.
Indeed, even sturdier singers who have worked in the

Corsaro production since Domingo left the company have paid mere lip service to the gesture; John Stewart, for example, picks Brooks up, then sets her down, and *then* begins to sing.

Domingo triumphed in this new production, and in a new Corsaro *Pagliacci* the following year, and the world began beating a path to his dressing room door. The year 1967 found him at the Hamburg Opera as Lohengrin, which is still his only foray into German opera aside from a recording of Weber's *Oberon*. Hamburg, one of the most adventurous of European houses in terms both of repertory and staging, had previously been the second home of other City Opera luminaries—the tenor Richard Cassilly, for example, and the soprano Arlene Saunders. And then, as must inevitably happen, the Metropolitan Opera's Rudolf Bing joined the path-beaters. Bing had been nursing a grudge against the City Opera since its move to Lincoln Center, feeling that that kind of competition at his own doorstep was a little close for comfort. At the same time, he soon came to recognize that there was more good than bad to be gained from such proximity, and—while he claimed ignorance at first hand of what was actually happening at the State Theater—he had begun what amounted to a lend-lease policy for talent with the junior company. In the fall of 1968, he tapped Domingo to cover for Franco Corelli in *Adriana Lecouvreur*, and also to take on a few performances of that work when Corelli was otherwise occupied. The debut was set for October 2, sandwiched into Domingo's continuing schedule at the City Opera across the way. But the debut actually occurred four days earlier, on September 28, when Corelli suddenly took ill, with consequences described earlier.

Domingo's Metropolitan Opera career began slowly but

ripened admirably. By the fall of 1969, he had begun singing first nights of productions, which means that the critics
heard him. He did not, however, cut his ties with Rudel and
the City Opera, although he did phase out his work there
somewhat. In October 1970, he was on hand in the title
role of the new production of Donizetti's *Roberto Devereux,*
as Beverly Sills began her traversal of the bel canto "Queens
Trilogy," and was generously noted amid the furore created
by the soprano. Aside from a few subsequent *Devereux*
performances, however, he has left the City Opera, and
not entirely without a sentimental backward glance. He
misses, in particular, the City Opera singers' attitude toward
rehearsals. "At the Met," he says, "everybody, or almost
everybody, tries to see how much he can get away with,
how many rehearsals he doesn't have to show up for, that
sort of thing. It's an attitude that rubs off, even when you
want to work hard. You look around, and see that nobody
else cares, and then you ask 'why should I be the only
one?' "

But 1969 was also the year of fruition on a broader scale.
It was the year of a La Scala debut, in a role (Ernani)
he had never sung before, and the year also of a London
debut, in a Verdi *Requiem* conducted by Giulini. The year
1970 witnessed a native son's return to Madrid, in a gala
*Gioconda,* TV recordings for the BBC, a *Don Carlo* in
Verona, and, a performance he treasures especially, a *Missa
Solemnis* in the Vatican attended by Pope Paul VI.

It was also the beginning of a career in the recording
studios, one that has become the most active and wide-
ranging of any tenor now active (Nicolaï Gedda, possibly,
excepted). Thanks in large measure to the triumphs of
Beverly Sills in rediscovered bel canto repertory, and before
her of Maria Callas and Joan Sutherland, a number of

major record companies reactivated their complete-opera projects, with particular attention accorded to out-of-the-way Italian romantic repertory: Bellini, Donizetti, and early works of Verdi—along with new versions of more familiar operas from the period. Domingo was, for many reasons, the perfect tenor to participate in these projects. For one thing, he has always been a quick study and a slow forgetter. But beyond that, the deep, pliant richness of his voice itself, and the massive control over it that he had been so carefully working out in the Tel Aviv years and beyond, qualified him uncommonly well to cope with the peculiar demands imposed by contemporary recording conditions. In any case, you'll look a long time before you'll find another tenor who, merely five years into an international career, is already represented by a dozen complete operas on major labels: Bellini's *Norma,* Verdi's *Aïda, Don Carlo, Lombardi, Trovatore, Giovanna d'Arco, Vespri Siciliani,* and the *Requiem;* Puccini's *Manon Lescaut* and *Tosca,* Leoncavallo's *Pagliacci,* Weber's *Oberon,* and Offenbach's *Les Contes d'Hoffmann*—plus a growing catalogue of single aria collections marketed under such titles as "Domingo Sings Caruso" and "La Voce d'Oro."

All this—the recordings, the international acclaim—had placed Domingo securely in the front ranks of star tenors, a fact not lost on the Metropolitan Opera. There are two ways the Met traditionally has of signalizing its respect for its stars—aside, of course, from paying them more money. One is a new production. That can be greatly important as a public attention-getter, and it also gives a performer the chance to create a character from the ground up, in a way that stepping into an older production, even in a shined-up revival, cannot. The other way is to accord that singer a seasonal opening night. The glamour of that assignment

may be harder to explain. Opening nights at the Met are
bound to be more social than artistic, and audiences in
the areas closest to the stage are always happiest when the
operas are short and undemanding. Nevertheless, opening
a season at the Met—or at La Scala or Covent Garden or
Vienna—seems to carry this inexplicable cachet, and it must
therefore he noted that, between 1971 and 1974, Domingo
was tapped for three out of four first-night performances.
The first was in the title role of *Don Carlo,* the opera that
had been Rudolf Bing's first production at the Met and
which, therefore, was selected to inaugurate his last season
at the house. The next, in '73, was as Manrico in *Il Trovatore,*
and the third, in '74, was as Arrigo in the company's new
production, its first ever, of Verdi's *I Vespri Siciliani.*

In 1973–74 also came Domingo's first new production
at the Met, and it turned out to be truly his. It was *Les*

Placido Domingo as Hoffmann in Offenbach's *Les Contes d'Hoffmann,*
with Huguette Tourangeau (*seated*) as Nicklausse (*Photo by Erika Davidson*)

*Contes d'Hoffmann,* in which the conductor, Richard Bonynge, had reconstructed a new version closer to Offenbach's original than the versions usually heard, and with Bonynge's wife, Joan Sutherland, cast as the four heroines. (This is the same version that appears, with Sutherland and Domingo, on the London recording.) Not all the critics were taken with the rather busy, murky production Domingo suffered in being forced throughout the opera to serve both as a spectator, at a table on the sidelines, and a participant; he was made to appear all night in the drab student costume of the Prologue. But the critics were unanimous on one point: that he had proven worthy of the task. Although the reception somewhat alleviated his personal distaste for the production, he prefers not to talk about it.

He prefers to discuss another new production now on the drawing boards, a long overdue Met revival tentatively set for 1976–77, of Meyerbeer's *L'Africaine,* in which he had brought down the house in San Francisco in the 1972–73 season. Schuyler Chapin had flown out to see the work, and both he and Domingo had come back to New York aglow.

One other major event in Domingo's growing career took place during the 1973–74 season, his formal debut as a conductor. Despite his long training with Markevitch, Domingo had not done any public work on the podium since the early days with the zarzuela company in Mexico. He had satisfied himself at rehearsals of the recorded collaboration with Milnes that he had the knack, but he had led the orchestra on that occasion with considerable trepidation. But the big chance came in the fall of 1973 at the New York City Opera. The company had opened its season a month late after a long musicians' strike, and many of its members, despairing of any season at all, had accepted other assignments. When the season finally began, therefore, there were a few holes in its schedule. One vacancy consisted of the lack of a conductor for a Sunday matinee of *La Traviata* early in October, and someone in the company suddenly got the bright notion of asking Domingo to help out his former colleagues. Despite a *Trovatore* at the Met on Friday night, and an *Adriana Lecouvreur* with the New Jersey Opera the following Monday, Domingo consented.

Things went very well, indeed. The usual backstage turmoil at the State Theater made it impossible to hold a complete orchestral rehearsal, but Domingo did have the chance to rehearse with his singers, among whom was his former partner, Patricia Brooks. And, despite the lack of full rehearsal, the neophyte conductor did make his mark on the overall performance. Visitors who trooped backstage to congratulate Domingo afterward also noted the presence of groups of orchestral musicians, discussing with surprise and respect the way he had pulled off some *diminuendo* or other. Among the others pleased with the results was Domingo himself. In the 1974–75 season he plans to conduct another Verdi opera, *Attila,* this time at Barcelona. And this time with rehearsals.

Relaxing in his suite at the St. Moritz Hotel a few days after the *Hoffmann* premiere, Domingo was in a jovial mood. The reviews had been kind toward him; he had, therefore, become reconciled to the many curiosities in the production. The hernia that had been plaguing him during rehearsals was now under control, and there was talk of a new diet to prevent a recurrence. Marta was off at the Domingo home, a rambling, comfortable place in suburban Teaneck, New Jersey, which was now being sold. Like so many other artists who divide their time between the United States and abroad, the Domingos have discovered the dollar advantage of European residency and, for this and a few other, more sentimental, reasons, are building a new home outside Barcelona.

Listening to Domingo talk about himself and his artistic outlook, it's easy to forget the old saw about tenors being the least intelligent wing of an opera company—a fact sometimes facetiously explained as coming from pressure on the brain caused by the tenor's particular vocal range. Domingo is not set apart from his colleagues by any marked degree of modesty; he knows how good he is, and how he got where he is today. But that's basic knowledge for any successful musician, and Domingo knows some other things, too. People close to him speak with some awe about his encyclopedic knowledge of the operatic repertory, works that he has sung as well as works that he hasn't, and also about his fabulous knowledge of his musical forebears, gleaned from long hours of studiously listening to records.

He does this listening, however, more for intellectual study than as a shortcut for his own training. "When I hear Caruso," he says, "I try to absorb the power that he had. Nobody could hit those top notes—the A's, the B-flats—the way he did. If I try to imitate Caruso's voice, then I, too, seem to have that power. But, then, it isn't my voice. As far as pure beauty, I much prefer Bjoerling, or the younger di Stefano, but even they didn't have the power, and the legato that comes from it, the way Caruso did."

We discussed that other old saw, whether Caruso's qualities would be valued if he were singing today the way he sang on records. "Yes, I'm sure that his greatness would still be recognized. I'm not so sure about other singers—Gigli, for example. In America, at least, he would have to control that sob.

"But that brings up that whole question about interpretation. Here at the Met, or in San Francisco, audiences seem to demand a clean, dry style of singing. They become uncomfortable at the notion of a tenor using a little extra expression, a sob or a little extra breath on a note. But when I sing in Europe, in Italy in particular, I make some changes. I can be freer. Take, for example, Turiddu in *Cavalleria Rusticana*. If you sing this part in an Italian house, most of the audience knows about the personality of this kind of fellow: he's a Sicilian, which already makes him very emotional; he's a little drunk; he's really frightened that Alfio may kill him. And so, it's perfectly natural that he will sob. It's part of the life-style in that country. Look. If I'm sitting in a hotel lobby in America and my father comes in, we will stand up and shake hands. In Italy, we would kiss. It's the same way with different ways of singing in the two countries.

"There are other differences, too, between singing in New York and singing abroad. At this moment, at least, New York is a soprano town. This current madness for sopranos began with the American Opera Society [a defunct organization that gave concert performances, mostly of forgotten *bel canto* works, in Carnegie Hall with great sopranos in the leading roles and your brother-in-law singing the other parts.] They brought in Callas, Sutherland, Horne, and Souliotis for their debuts, Sills, and so forth. People went crazy over these stars, and forgot everyone else. This is an obsession that ought to be changed, and I hope I can help, because it means that people aren't listening to the whole of opera, just certain parts."

We moved on to the matter of repertory. "The more I work, the more I am convinced that Verdi is the composer for my voice. Sure, I like to do some of the *verismo* operas, and I think you are all wrong in the things you have written about *Adriana Lecouvreur*. Yes, there are some things wrong with the music, but it is very generously written to give the tenor the chance to act with his voice—much more so than *Cav* and *Pag*.

"That is the most important thing for me, to be able to act with my voice. I know I don't move around the stage like a dancer, but I don't think I'm bad, either. But that is not as important to me as bringing out the action strictly by singing it. Take a part like Radames, for example, in *Aïda*. This is a very strong, dramatic role, that takes a good deal of movement. But I approach Radames as basically a lyric role, not much different from Manrico or Riccardo. If you don't have that throb in the throat, it doesn't matter how much dancing around you can do on the stage.

"You ask me to describe my own voice . . . you know, I've never thought about that before. I suppose I think of a cello as the ideal; yes, I would rather think of it that way. Some people come up to me and they say that I sound like Caruso, or that I sound like him in some particular spot. But that doesn't interest me, because I don't even *want* to sound like Caruso. Di Stefano, Bjoerling, Gigli . . . perhaps. But all I want is to make the most beautiful legato, with a sound a little like golden honey—or, like a cello.

"Let's put it another way. I think of myself as a tenor with a certain amount of voice, quite a large amount, actually. But then the problem is to color that voice, to change it for different roles, or for different moments. In 1975 I will sing Otello, which is another role that is usually considered more dramatic than lyric. Actually, it is a role with more than one color, and a great deal of it is lyric. In the 'Sì, pel ciel' duet you have to be dramatic, but the 'Esultate!' and the 'Ora e per sempre' . . . those are lyric, or spinto, moments. After Otello I might be tempted by some more German roles: Lohengrin again, and Walther in

*Die Meistersinger,* and, perhaps some day, Tristan. Tristan, too, is basically a lyric role, but it is a dangerous one. Most of it lies in the middle tessitura, and if you have to sing lyrically around an F or an F-sharp, you have to be very careful; that can really tire your voice. That's why Tristans are so hard to find: not because of any shortage of *helden-tenors,* but rather because of a shortage of lyric tenors with the proper kind of strength.

"German opera can ruin your voice, but *any* opera can ruin your voice if you don't have the proper training, and the sense to know what you're singing. Every tenor loves to sing Andrea Chénier, because they think it's such a grateful role for the voice. But there's a swelling on a middle D at the end of the 'Improvviso' in that opera that can absolutely wreck your voice forever. A singer with a bad technique can 'get through' *verismo* opera—although he can lose his voice in the process—but he can never get through Verdi or Donizetti.

"People also ask me all the time: 'What do you do, as a *Spanish* tenor, that is different from being an Italian, or some other, tenor?' Actually, there is a great deal of confusion about this business of nationality. I am a Spanish tenor because I was born in Spain, but I grew up in Mexico and studied with an Italian. The color of a voice has nothing to do with nationality. Bjoerling had the real Latin quality in his voice, but he was born in Sweden. The color in your voice doesn't come from the language you speak at home; it comes from the language you're singing in the opera house. Sure, if I sing Don José in *Carmen* I may have a little special insight, because my mother comes from the same part of Spain where José was born. But that's just an accident, and the role is not written in Spanish, but French, and by a French composer."

Conversation turned to the matter of recordings, a not

inconsiderable matter in the life of a singer who is now one of the best sellers among tenors, whose royalties from one company alone (RCA, where he is now under exclusive contract) have long since passed the six-figure mark. "Records are important to me, but more for economic than artistic reasons. They are a little like a trust fund. But I am never happy with a recorded performance, because I am still young and still in a process of change. Thank God nobody recorded the way I was singing Manrico, for example, six or seven years ago, because I have totally changed the vocal color of that role—as I have for almost everything I sing. But also, I prefer the sound of old recordings, even the acoustic ones, to the sort of thing that is done nowadays, where everything is made so perfect, so hi-fi, in the studios. Stereo recording has spoiled the purity of the singer, because everything is done with the microphone. On the old records, a singer gave his complete power, so that Caruso, for example, sounds on records a lot closer to the way he sounded in performance than I think I do on my records. It's strange; in the studio we are always excited by what we have just done, but it never sounds that way when we hear it. We also develop terrible habits by knowing that the engineers can always fix a bad spot by splicing the tape. I think the best way to make a recording would be, either to record a live performance on the stage or, at least, to invite an audience into the studio.

"If I could build an opera house, and hire the greatest singers of the past to perform there, my company would include Caruso and Gigli, of course, Flagstad, Muzio, Ponselle, Ruffo, Stracciari, and Chaliapin. My conductors, however, would be from the present: Jimmy Levine and—this may surprise you—Nello Santi. I know that Santi had a very bad career at the Met, but I admire his conducting because

Placido Domingo (*Photo by Erika Davidson*)

it seems to be very much in the tradition of the older singers, and he has a great regard for the old vocal traditions—as, you see, I do.

"Enough, however, of the past and the present. I've done quite a lot of thinking about the future, too. I suppose you could say I started thinking about times ahead last season at the Met, when I went on in a *Trovatore* and cracked on the high note in 'Di quella pira.' That was a bad time. I was sick, first of all, and the Met simply didn't have anyone covering me. I shouldn't have gone on at all. I realize that cracking on one note, even if you know it's the most exciting note in the whole opera, means nothing, or *should* mean nothing. But I also have to remember that there is a certain part of every audience, at every house, who comes to an opera the way the Romans went to watch Christians being thrown to the lions. That night the lions dined well.

"Anyhow, I started thinking. If I crack on one note now and then, it means nothing. But what happens when I start cracking on two notes, then three, then four. I hope I will recognize that day, and be able to say to myself, 'Placido, no more' before the audience says it for me.

"When that time comes, I will be ready. First of all, I will keep on with my conducting. It's very important to me that we're going back to Spain, to live near Barcelona, because I want to be involved with the opera house there. It's the only real house in Spain, you know. I also want my children to grow up speaking their own language. Then, I want to start a little zarzuela troupe like my parents'—here in New York. There is a huge Spanish-speaking population here, and they deserve to hear their own theatrical tradition. I would be happy to sing with this company, in less demanding roles, of course. And I would also like to sing some pop songs, not because of furthering my own career, but because

I really enjoy singing light music. After all, Caruso sang Neapolitan songs."

Considering the present state of the Domingo career, plans for semiretirement into zarzuela and pop should materialize somewhere around 2001. Some of his friends aren't too sure, however; the fear most often expressed about his work these days is that he sings too much, over too wide a range, and in too many places. Domingo has a stock answer for this, one that was even used as the title for a *New York Times* profile on him a couple of years ago: "The more I sing, the better I sound." It is true, of course, that jet planes have made possible schedules for singers these days that would have staggered anyone in any other golden age. But the great Lotte Lehmann had an interesting comment on overwork in a radio interview a while back. "It's true," she said, "that singers today perform more often than we used to, and that many of them wear themselves out. But if you ask me if I would have done the same thing in my day if jet planes had been invented, I would have to answer 'yes.'"

Domingo has the sense, at least, to recognize the problem. He has begun to phase out his appearances, at the Met and in other houses, to a maximum of two well-spaced performances a week—avoiding a repetition of a time when he would sing *Forza* on a Saturday night and *Luisa Miller* the following Monday, or, for that matter, of the Saturday when he sang a matinee performance and then replaced an ailing tenor in the evening. "That was madness," he explains quite simply. His current routine before a performance is to see a bad movie the night before, sleep late the day of the performance, eat a steak at 2 P.M., and sleep some more until curtain time, a sensible routine free of the mumbo jumbo that singers used to announce about themselves to a waiting press. While on the stage, he willingly admits, he derives further nourishment from applause.

"Sometimes I think I'm old-fashioned," he says. "But when I've really sung well on a night—at the Met, or in Vienna, or at La Scala, anywhere—and the audience stays behind at the final curtain to let me know I've been all right, that's when I really want to start singing. If I was in charge of the opera house, and if we didn't have a stage-hands' union to protest, I'd wheel out a piano at that point and sing all night. That's all I really want to do: just sing."

Nice guys, you see, don't *always* finish last.

# Luciano Pavarotti

BY

*Stephen E. Rubin*

TRADITIONALLY speaking, the most accurate one-word description of the singular species *tenore italiano* might well be: Fat. Luciano Pavarotti, a *tenore italiano* if there ever was one, gives the tradition a new dimension. Weighing in at over 300 pounds, the singer is considerably more amplitudinous than his fleshy forebears. But Pavarotti is no ordinary ho-ho-ho fat man; he is a monster-sized rascal, content in his corpulence, who gleefully thumbs his stomach at the universe.

His is the perfect marriage of mind and body. As he is physically immense, so is he personally larger than life. Pavarotti's is a cosmos unto itself, a realm bursting with superlatives. It is no coincidence that friends call him *Lucianissimo* or that Joan Sutherland affectionately refers to him as Big P.

If all the world is a stage, then Pavarotti is its biggest ham. He is always on, always up; if there are, as there must be, depressive moments to balance the manic ones, he is gloomy in private. Even when nervous or upset, Pavarotti generally acts his way out of an uncomfortable situation. He is the eternal performer, and if his steamer trunk full of tricks run short, he is never at a loss to improvise. An hour and a half before his first Metropolitan Nemorino (in *L'Elisir d'Amore*), a role he relishes but admits is difficult to bring off convincingly, the tenor was busily learning Fauré songs in his dressing room. Teaching him was his coach and accompanist Eugene Kohn who, on important occasions like this one, often tries to unwind Pavarotti by giving him new material to master. But the student was fidgety, and the session worked only moderately.

The tenor was happy because he unearthed a bent nail on stage—Italian for good luck—but miserable because his peasant's costume was too *large* for him. In between putting on makeup and learning Fauré, he would call for his dresser, an elderly gent who was forever disappearing. "This costume is for me and my daughter!" he cried melodramatically. "No, it is not too late to fix," he said patiently. "You just move the buttons." Off went the dresser to the costume mistress. Fifteen minutes later when there was no sign of him, off went Pavarotti into the hallway and, instead of throwing a tenor tantrum, he sang the man's name *fortissimo* until he reappeared.

Two hours before a TV talk-show guest spot, Pavarotti was warned that he had to climb five steep flights to reach a dressing room. Without wasting a moment, the tenor fled directly to the producer and, oozing charm, voiced a deeply felt concern that the journey might do Kohn (who is in his mid-twenties and the picture of health) great harm. You see, Pavarotti reported sadly, he has a heart condition and is very weak. When this obvious ploy failed, the annoyed guest begrudgingly took the steps very slowly, muttering colorful Italian profanities under his breath.

Usually Pavarotti gets his way, and not because of childish displays of pique or superstar terror tactics He is much too shrewd to employ a negative approach when he knows that, in his case, the positive pitch will almost always succeed. He knows—in much the same way that you knew that Cary Grant knew that he would get the girl. Pavarotti has a similar, if less subtle, kind of charm—easy, natural, irresistible, and as penetrating as a laser beam. The tenor is also endlessly resourceful, shamelessly nervy, exceedingly clever, and appealingly childlike. In short, he has all the traits of a spoiled brat. That he is lovable instead is a tribute to his innate instinct for good taste just this side of Italian extravagance.

That he has made these instincts work for him, both in the theater and in life, proves that along with his other assets there is also intelligence. As tenors go, Pavarotti is a genius. He has common sense, native intelligence—all the phrases that imply a good mind, but not necessarily intellect. This is probably just as well; too much cerebral inquisitiveness would no doubt inflict irreparable damage to an art whose glory is its natural and unaffected grace and beauty.

In this sense, Pavarotti is far removed from what has come to be known as a German, or thinking man's tenor. But neither is he a typical whining, sobbing, belching, burping, pigheaded Italian tenor. Pavarotti is a well-grounded musician who phrases with finesse and lands on a note directly without employing scoops or slides to get there. Because he is singing with ease, his enunciation of the text is as crystal clear as his pitch is dead-center precise. "He is my favorite kind of musician," coach Kohn reports, "in that he didn't study sixteenth notes, and doesn't read off the page like a million bucks. Rather, he feels the music instinctively, and his instincts are almost always correct. This, to me, is really great musicianship."

Like his countrymen, Pavarotti means business and is out to milk every last ounce of applause—often going as far as having it clocked—but none of his pizzazz is displayed at the expense of the music. Soprano Beverly Sills tells of the time they were singing *I Puritani* together and had decided beforehand that, no matter what, there would be no taking of bows after either arias or duets, a custom observed in Europe. "But when it came to the end of the fourth-act duet, the audience was screaming," Miss Sills recalls, "and Luciano kept on looking at me as though to say 'let's take a bow.' I kept looking at him and shaking my head no. Finally, he gave me a great big bear hug and kissed me on my shoulder, which of course got even more applause. As we walked offstage, he glanced at me coyly and said, 'Ah, but I didn't bow!'"

Obviously, Pavarotti is no musical or theatrical saint. It is purely by comparison to the idiot tenor of legend that he shines like a knight. The singer respects the printed notes and the men who wrote them as well as the maestros in the pit whom, he feels, are the true leaders, the greatest source of inspiration. In this belief, he is in direct opposition to an unfortunate Italian tradition which dictates that the singer is paramount, the music is secondary, and the conductor is a necessary evil. Curiously, it is his knowing mixture of the best from the past and the best from today that makes him the unique hybrid he is. His bulk surely harks back to when singers were called cows for good reason. His voice, too, is of a variety that is uncommon these days. There may be some tenors who can squeeze out a D-flat, but few can reach the note while still keeping the sound as clear and pure as Pavarotti does. As conductor Thomas Schippers says, "A boxer with bellows like that is unfair to other singers."

His acting abilities are nowhere near as elegant as his vocalizing. But by operatic standards, he is more than acceptable. Surprisingly, he moves onstage with a bouncy grace rare to men of his size. Subtlety is not yet within his grasp, but believability is. "The old tradition where the singer is standing and singing is definitely finished," Pavarotti proclaims. He credits his dramatic verisimilitude to the simple fact that "I believe what I do. Absolutely. No matter which role."

This sincerity—perhaps the first and foremost aspect of

Luciano Pavarotti (*left*) as Riccardo with Sherrill Milnes as Renato in Verdi's *Un Ballo in Maschera* (*Hamburg State Opera*)

his art to travel across the footlights—is the essential ingre-
dient of his mastery in not only holding the audience's
attention, but in making it totally sympathetic to both
Luciano Pavarotti and the character he is playing. The
tenor realizes that he has this ability but cannot, under-
standably, define it. "I don't see me, so I cannot say," he
says. "But I can tell you that Georg Solti came to see
*Daughter of the Regiment* at Covent Garden and after-
wards he said to me, 'Luciano, you can sing the telephone
book, because when you come out you have something
inside I cannot explain, but everybody is with you.' I cannot
explain it either. I don't know what it is."

What it is is star quality, that magical spell which tran-
scends a given art form and becomes all-encompassing.
Garbo was as tantalizing offscreen as on. Olivier is a figure
of stature in a walk-on part. Bernstein is as dazzling a man
as he is a maestro. Callas makes headlines whether she
sings or not.

Pavarotti is not yet in this class of legends; he is merely a
superstar. But he is on his way. So far, he has conquered
the opera and recital stages—in itself rare for an Italian
tenor. Anyone who has seen him on a TV talk show realizes
that he is a natural in this guise, even when chatting in
English, with which he is comfortable but hardly eloquent.
Films should be next, and if they work, there is no telling
what is in the future. Since he is fearless, there is literally
no limit. The point is that Pavarotti is primarily a personality
who happens also to be a superb singer.

As such, he is the hottest tenor in the business. Early in
1974, he had an unheard of five albums on *Billboard*'s best-
selling classical LP chart. Two of them, *Turandot* and *La
Bohème*, were numbers one and two. Pavarotti has his com-
petitors, but the only tenor singing his repertory who begins

to match him today is Placido Domingo, a different kind of singer with a different kind of voice, who can also drum up plenty of excitement, but not of the frenzy level that is Pavarotti's alone.

No blowhard, the artist is loath to admit his preeminent position today. He will speak openly around the subject, though. "About two years ago [1971], I decided to be a really professional singer and become very famous around the world by going to the people who cannot come to me and doing recitals," Pavarotti explains. "It's a hard life, but what is easy, you tell me? It's also a great big responsibility, and I accept it. I cannot be without it; I like it very much. It is really a part of myself already. It's like some drug. For example, if you drink Campari, you cannot stop because of something inside of you. Coca-Cola is the same. I can't talk about real drugs because I never tried them, but I suppose it's something like that. Once you begin you cannot stop.

"If you consider that I was born in a family where everyone was singing 'Di quella pira,' my mother, father, grandmother, you can understand that the responsibility of my job is very heavy, but not a big pain. It's very good to have this. It's exactly what I was looking for when I was born. It's so natural for me, not complicated."

Perhaps one of the reasons that being a celebrity comes easily to the tenor is that he makes little or no effort to separate the offstage and onstage Pavarotti. Gene Kohn, who travels with him constantly, believes that "he hides nothing in his private life. When we were in Italy once, we went to a *trattoria* in the mountains. I was sure no one would recognize him. But a few minutes after we sat down, a bottle of Luciano's favorite wine was sent to the table, compliments of some people in the restaurant who wrote that he was their favorite tenor. Luciano immediately invited them over to our table, and we spent the entire evening together as though they were his best friends. He's beautiful in that way. He wants his life and career to be one, and he's very generous in wanting to share it with others."

Almost simplistically, Pavarotti says, "The only complicated part of my life is for me to be very good, at the top, every night. This is very difficult, impossible. I hope I keep a high standard. My job is over all other things. There is not one minute of doubt about that!"

Pavarotti means what he says despite the fact that he is married and has three young daughters. He spends far more time talking about his family than being with them. Signora Pavarotti, the former Adua Veroni, occasionally travels with her husband, but for the most part is home with the kids on the outskirts of Modena—the tenor's birthplace—in a large house she shares with her sister, brother-in-law, and four nephews. The star of the family is part of the mélange three or four weeks a year as well as an odd, quick visit here and there.

If this setup causes him any pain, he rarely speaks about it, except tangentially. He knows that a life of constant travel, of often being lonely is what he has cut out for himself. But his deep familial feelings can sometimes get the best of him. In 1965, for the first month of a fourteen-week tour of Australia with Joan Sutherland, Mrs. Pavarotti accompanied her husband. When it came time for her to leave, the tenor escorted his wife to the airport and, back in his hotel room, fell into a black slump. "I was so unhappy," Pavarotti recalls. "I kept thinking, now she has a thirty-hour plane trip. We had two daughters then, and I started thinking about them and what would happen if the plane goes down.

"I didn't know what to do, so I started studying. I put on a record of the Verdi *Requiem* conducted by Giulini with Schwarzkopf, Ludwig, Gedda, and Ghiaurov. After five minutes, I was crying like a cow. All I could think of were planes going down. Never has music touched me like that. The *Requiem* is so true, and this performance of Giulini's is the most close to being the real thing that Verdi wanted."

"Pavarotti is greatly affected by and has a deep, deep respect of death," Eugene Kohn says. "He's always concerned about the health and safety of his children. In fact, I enjoy him most when he's around his family because he's more relaxed, less on. When he's home in Modena, his singing is also more tender, as if he has less to worry about."

Terry McEwen, vice-president in charge of the classical division of London Records, the company for which Pavarotti records, and a close friend of the tenor, explains his preoccupation with death differently. McEwen, who is not quite as large as Pavarotti, but comes close, feels that an understanding of the "fat man's syndrome" can illuminate his behavior. "Luciano, like all of us fat men, doesn't expect to live to a ripe old age," the record executive says, "and he wants to confirm his immortality by making records, singing roles, giving concerts. There is always the feeling, which I understand, that he hasn't got too much time."

The human voice being what it is, singers—fearful of death or not—tend to be somewhat unstable. They know, as everybody else knows, that tomorrow it could be all over. Pavarotti is secure enough, however, to give others their due, to enjoy the triumphs of his colleagues, and always to be a gentleman where they are concerned. Petty jealousies are not his style. Baritone Sherrill Milnes recalls the day after his Hamburg debut when Pavarotti congratulated him on having a front-page picture in the newspaper. "Luciano was also in the cast, and rather than thinking, well, who did you pay, he was very happy for me," Milnes reports.

Pavarotti even has a good word for a number of current tenors. Once, following the first act of a *Bohème* broadcast from the Metropolitan, the tenor was so excited by the performance of Richard Tucker, he impulsively phoned his colleague during the intermission. "I just can't believe it. I had to call you," he said hotly. "You're still the top tenor in the world, a phenomenon."

Tucker, a bit less effusive, returns some of the compliments. "I consider Luciano one of the most gifted of the young generation of singers, especially when it comes to lyrical singers," the veteran says. "He's a very sincere person and a good colleague. Whenever I sing at the Met, and know that he is going to occupy the dressing room after me, I write *buona fortuna* on the mirror with greasepaint."

To the young American tenor John Stewart, "the greatest thing about Pavarotti is that he makes it all look so easy. It's not so much an absence of nerves—he's clearly plenty concerned about certain high notes, the C-sharp in 'A te, o cara,' from *Puritani*, for example. But there is an absence of physical tensions—no gasping breath, hunching of shoulders, popping of neck veins, or wobbling of jaw. He opens his mouth (not too widely), and beautiful sound pours forth."

Following the release of his recording of *Turandot*, Pavarotti was like a child whose birthday falls on Christmas and had just received double presents from his entire family. The tenor had every reason to be euphoric; his Calaf is exceptional, as is the entire performance conducted by Zubin Mehta with Joan Sutherland, Montserrat Caballé, and Nicolai Ghiaurov.

Virtually jumping up and down, he asks: "How did you

Luciano Pavarotti as Fritz with Mirella Freni as Suzel in Mascagni's
*L'Amico Fritz* (*Photo Courtesy Angel Records*)

like the way Joan sang 'Sì, la speranza che delude sempre'?"
This is Turandot's sarcastic reply to Calaf's first correct
answer of the three riddles. Sutherland spits out the line
with an unusually chesty and exciting delivery. "You like,
eh?" he grins a mile wide. "Not bad, eh? I said to her, Joan,
you sing it this way and it'll be *fabalos*."

Pavarotti is one of those tenors who, instead of battling
with his leading ladies, loves them and they return the
compliment. He has probably sung with every major international prima donna except Birgit Nilsson, a fact which
he would like soon to remedy. Because of his alliance
with London Records, he has both recorded and performed
live a great deal with Miss Sutherland, whom he obviously
adores as an artist and a friend.

"He's just a big, lovable bandit," Miss Sutherland says
with an enormous giggle and knowing look. "Actually,
Luciano has a huge heart and he's very devoted to singing.
And, of course, he sings like an angel. But he scares the
hell out of me when I see him getting fatter and fatter,
although I'm a nice one to talk. At least when I get to a
certain level, I know I have to do something about it.
But Luciano's got this mad zest for eating."

The tenor owes much to the soprano and her husband,
Richard Bonynge. The Australian tour for which they engaged him in 1965, when he was hardly a known commodity, helped not only to establish him, but to grant him
much-needed experience. It was also the Bonynges who
brought him to London Records. With typical generosity,
Miss Sutherland denies any credit for his career. "Oh, come
on!" she explodes. "If I hadn't taken him to Australia,
dearie, someone would have taken him somewhere else. As
for London Records, we said he's here and he's fabulous.
But you can't hide that!"

Records are a vital part of a major singer's career today. It is virtually impossible to be internationally renowned without them. Pavarotti takes them very seriously, often to the point of being nervous and dissatisfied with his performances. And if he likes the way he sings, he doesn't like the acoustics or the way his voice has been reproduced. He is completely forthright when describing his first London solo recital as being "beautiful, but *un po'* the same," and is also aboveboard when he says of his interpretation of Riccardo in *Ballo in Maschera*, "I can do much better now. I recorded the part without singing it onstage first."

His more recent recorded efforts tend to be generally more satisfying, both from a vocal and interpretive viewpoint. He credits this to his experience in the studios. "When I made my first recordings in 1962, I was in top voice and the record was rubbish," he exclaims. "Why? Because I was an expert and did five arias in one afternoon, singing all the time when they weren't recording. *Stupido!* Sometimes now, when I'm not in great form, the record comes out still very good because I know what I have to do."

Indeed, and much to the distress of London Records. Terry McEwen claims that he has picked up what he calls a "Corelli characteristic" and is a little neurotic about his sound on records. "At a playback, he will listen to a chunk and say fine," McEwen reports. "Then, when we send him a test pressing, he says no, I'm flat. Getting a recital record out of him is like getting blood out of a stone. He's still so emotionally involved, he isn't able to coolly listen to playbacks. Our *Rigoletto* recording sat on the shelf for a year because of Luciano."

Pavarotti may have made a few mistakes in his professional life, but they are the exceptions in a career that has been very carefully and cleverly charted. While the tenor

has been able to retain a youthful and aggressive enthusiasm—often to the point of becoming tiresome—he has rarely
allowed the ardor of the moment to get the better of him.
Unlike so many of his jet-age colleagues, who burn their
candles on both ends by flying endlessly and singing too
frequently, he takes care of himself and his voice. Perhaps
most significantly, that unerring instinct of his has never
allowed him to become taken for granted because of overexposure. He may well have learned this trick from Joan
Sutherland whose handling of her career could be studied
as a perfect model of control and moderation.

When one is constantly in demand all over the world, the
discipline involved in knowing when, where, and how to say
no can be very trying. Pavarotti and his managers have
obviously acquired the knack. He is booked solid—and
would be furious if he weren't—but within the bounds of
good sense. This logical strain, in an often illogical and
crazy world, is something Pavarotti was nurtured on. He did
not reach his current status by jumping full-grown into the
den of lions that is the international operatic circuit today.
It was gradually that he developed into the number-one
gladiator.

It also took him time to master some of the facts of life.
"As a boy, I was very innocent, a little stupid," he recalls.
"If a friend would walk over to me and say, listen, we have
two moons tonight, I'd say okay. I've become a little more
clever now, because my life is totally different. But I really
haven't changed at all, except in experience. I'm still like a
child inside, with experience, but ready to have every new
sensation from the world. I like people very much and I
want to meet them. My wife is jealous because of this. She
thinks I like the girls. That's not the point. I like the
people."

Such was little Luciano's love of "the people," he was probably Modena's biggest gossip. "We lived in a house on the limit of the city called Casa Populare. It was poor, but clean and free because there was much ground. There were sixteen families there with fifty boys. I knew what was happening in all sixteen of them, between everybody. The women put the laundry outside, and I knew which hand-kerchief belonged to whom. I was a very big observer.

"My oldest daughter is the same as I was. If a person comes to visit us, after three minutes, she tells you exactly what that person is like. She began doing this when she was four. She is a child in feeling, but not in mind, the same way I was. At six, I was thinking exactly like I'm thinking now. My second daughter is a little like her, but the third is just a child."

Pavarotti, who was born in 1935, speaks of his youth in Modena with great relish, often becoming carried away with happy memories and tending to exaggerate. There is no doubt though that his was a lively and buoyant child-hood. "All my character comes from that period," he an-nounces. Luciano's father was and still is a baker, and his mother was employed in a tobacco factory making cigars. Because both his parents worked, he had great freedom and was in no way averse to taking advantage of it.

"I was a wild boy, very nice but very wild, not sleepy," he reports. "I was never, never inside. My mother and father saw me just when I was eating and sleeping. Other-wise, I was playing soccer and all other sports, ten hours a day minimum. You know, in Italy soccer is the most popular sport. I was very good, and played for my city. I don't understand how one can be excited about baseball. It's boring. Football is much better. But for soccer you must be very intelligent, because you can't use your hands."

As a fitting change of pace for the lad, when he wasn't getting his shins bloodied on the playing field, he was planted in front of the looking glass engaged in a different kind of exercise. "The mirror was my best friend," he laughs. "I stood there all the time singing 'La donna e mobile,' and 'di quella pira.' Why not? Everybody in my country did that at the age of six or seven. The TV wasn't invented yet. The opera was the most important thing in our city. We have a very beautiful theater for 1,300 people, which has perfect acoustics. It was made in the old style, like La Scala, Venice, Naples, and Bologna. We have perhaps more than one hundred theaters in Italy like that.

"For us, opera is in the blood. I can't remember, but it was either Toscanini or Verdi who, when asked by a conductor what the tempo of a certain piece was, said, 'Go to Parma. Hear the laundry lady on the river. This is the right tempo.'"

Pavarotti had it easier. He didn't have to go anywhere. In his own home, there was the perfect catalyst to make a little boy's throat itch to sing. His father, Fernando, was and still is, in the son's words, "a fantastic tenor." Pavarotti likens his father's voice to Galliano Masini, a popular Italian tenor. "I don't want to give him too much credit," he says continuing, "but the color of my father's voice was between Gigli's and Caruso's. It is a short voice, B-natural is the maximum, but very strong, open, natural, and exciting like you cannot imagine."

Why didn't the elder Pavarotti sing professionally if he was so good? "Because if he see somebody in front of him, he die," the son answers simply. "And when you are afraid, the first thing you lose is the diaphragm, and if you lose that you lose everything."

And so papa Pavarotti had to settle for singing in the

Modena church choir (behind the altar), and with him he brought his son, a mere tot of four. For ten years the boy sang alto, then his voice broke and he was forced to take a twenty-four-month sabbatical. At sixteen, he was back in the choir business again, both in church and as one of the eighty-five members of Modena's all-male Rossini chorus. The group was good enough to travel and enter competitions, but for his first two years Luciano was not among the members chosen to partake in the field trips. In 1955, however, his time came and off he went to England, along with his father and twenty other Rossinians to compete against eighteen choruses.

"I can never forget this," Pavarotti sighs. "There were 12,000 people at the competition. Each chorus sang two obligatory pieces and one free choice. I had been warned that the English people would not give first prize to a foreign group. But we sang so beautifully, I said to my father, it is impossible to sing better than we have. Let's see what happens, he said. And we won! Everybody was crying. I am touched now thinking of it. It was one of the greatest experiences of my life, including those of my solo career. When we went home, a band was at the station waiting for us, and all the streets of the city were full of flowers. It was wonderful."

There is nothing like a taste of public adoration, however small, to whet the appetite of an inveterate ham for more of the same. At this period, Pavarotti had already graduated from the Scuola delle Magistralle and was a full-fledged elementary schoolteacher. He was responsible for all the subjects taught to boys between the ages of six and eleven. "I enjoyed it very much," he says of his days as an instructor. "I think I was very good in the sense of teaching boys what they have to learn, but I was also very inflexible and sometimes used my hands. A boy must be your friend and must accept the hand. I liked the contact with children, but do you know how much they pay me? *Eight dollars a month!* Is that good? You like this, eh?"

Money wasn't the only problem. There were other forces gnawing at Pavarotti. One day, in 1955, he confronted his father and said: "I have finished my schooling and I am a teacher of children. Tell me if you want me to continue, or if you want me to study to become a tenor. My father said, 'It's very difficult. One million start and only one arrives.' And then my mother said, 'I think it's better if you try because, when you sing, your voice touches me.' And so I began to study."

After two years, he left the elementary school and became an insurance salesman in an effort to gain money, time and to save his voice. "Talking very much is worse than singing very much," he says. He studied diligently, both in Modena and in Mantua, but found the process exasperating. "In my country, voice is the only thing," he explains. "It is hard to find the right balance. There are a lot of singers with beautiful voices and no heart. And there are a lot of singers with no voices and plenty of heart. To try to have both is very difficult. You must be very careful. I am still waiting for perfection, which will never happen in my life. I don't even find it in others, so I surely won't find it in myself. But to try to drive the voice in the right place and to be more artistic than is possible is the dream."

Although Pavarotti speaks hyperbolically, it is not idle exaggeration. He kids constantly, teases, and makes jokes, but on the subject of his striving to become a greater total artist, he is dead serious. He worked very hard as a singing student and, in 1961, at the age of twenty-five, entered and won the Concorso Internationale Competition in the nearby town of Reggio nell'Emilia. The victory meant an engagement with the local opera house as Rodolfo in *La Bohème*.

"Francesco Molinari-Pradelli was the conductor for nothing and Mafalda Favero was the *régisseur* for nothing," he recalls. "It was a great experience, so beautiful and exciting. For fifteen days we stayed together, actually living like Bohemians. At the end, just before the performance, I was more nervous to see the face of Molinari-Pradelli than the public. I was afraid of him very much. After 'Che gelida manina' at the dress rehearsal, he stop the orchestra and say, 'Eh, young boy, you sing like that tomorrow night, you break down the theater!' For a person like him, this is a big phrase." Did he sing like that at the performance? "Oh, yes. And after this, he was not so nice with me. He was jealous."

Since this historic occasion in Pavarotti's life, he has always insisted on making his major debuts as Rodolfo. He came to the Metropolitan in *La Bohème*, as well as to Covent Garden, San Francisco, Chicago, Buenos Aires, La Scala, and Vienna.

The year 1961 was also significant because of his marriage, after an eight-year engagement, to Adua Veroni, whom he had met when they were both studying to become schoolteachers. Mrs. Pavarotti continued at her trade for a while after their marriage until she settled down to become a full-time mother. Her husband is fond of reporting that for ten days following the wedding ceremony, she supported him. Then he had his first real professional engagement, as the Duke in *Rigoletto*, at Carpi, a small community not far from Modena, and he was on his way, both as breadwinner and tenor. There followed a number of some smallish and two major—Venice and Palermo—assignments in Italy and elsewhere and then, in 1963, he had a great stroke of luck.

He was invited by Covent Garden to stand by in case

Giuseppe di Stefano, a tenor not noted for his reliability, failed to show up for rehearsals of a new production of *La Bohème*. Di Stefano lived up to his reputation, and Pavarotti got to sing the whole run of performances. In itself, this was fortunate. But the snowballing effect it had, in essence, established him. Joan Sutherland heard him at the Garden, and the experience prompted her and her husband to invite him to join their Australian tour of 1965. During those fourteen weeks, he not only sang in *La Traviata, La Sonnambula,* and *L'Elisir d'Amore,* he also mastered English, being forced to speak the language with his colleagues, the Bonynges, Elizabeth Harwood, John Alexander and Spiro Malas.

His American debut, in San Francisco, followed the next year, which also saw him at La Scala singing the Verdi *Requiem* for the first time in a performance under Herbert von Karajan honoring the centenary of Toscanini's birth.

Luciano Pavarotti (*left*) as Tonio, Joan Sutherland as Marie, and Fernando Corena as Sulpice in Donizetti's *La Fille du Régiment* (**Photo by Louis Mélançon**)

In 1968, Pavarotti came to the Met. The debut was completely successful, but it was not until 1972, when he sang Tonio in *Daughter of the Regiment*, that he became a Met superstar.

This is curious. Earlier, Harold C. Schonberg in *The New York Times* had endorsed him heartily as having "a golden-age voice." The public, too, warmed up by his recordings and word-of-mouth on the gossipy operatic circuit, was cheering him. And yet, it took Tonio, and an enormous amount of accompanying publicity, to put him right up there among the Met's biggies.

All the more peculiar, and a paean to Pavarotti's theatrical magic, is the fact that *Daughter of the Regiment* is usually the soprano's show. This is not to say that Miss Sutherland, with whom he sang, was in any way in the shadow of her tenor. On the contrary, they played to one another like a veteran comedy team. But when Pavarotti sang his aria with its nine high C's, pandemonium broke loose. He also acted the bumpkin to the hilt and got laughs from the moment he entered wearing an outrageous costume. It was a great show on the part of all concerned, but somehow without Pavarotti it had less panache.

The tenor chooses the roles he sings carefully, and not only because of purely vocal considerations. Whenever possible, he wants a showcase for his histrionic as well as vocal abilities. He goes about picking and choosing in a manner that is decidedly logical, if somewhat blunt and against the dictates of tradition. He will never sing Otello, for example, whether he believes he could portray the Moor or not. The part is obviously too heavy for his voice. But he would be content never again to sing Alfredo in *La Traviata* either, and it lies perfectly for him.

"I don't like to do *Traviata* because it is the soprano's

opera," Pavarotti says wisely. "The baritone comes out and sings a beautiful *duetto,* then has a fat aria, and he gets all the applause. He's the second person of the night. Violetta is first. And Alfredo with his stupid character is last."

*Faust* for Pavarotti is even worse. "The more I see this opera onstage, the more I realize that the first role belongs to Mefistofele, the second to the lady, and the third to the tenor. And Faust's aria, 'Salut! demeure chaste et pure,' is very incredibly boring!"

Pavarotti has misgivings about another vocally perfect part for him, the Duke in *Rigoletto,* but here the problem is completely dramatic, and one he seems to have mastered. "The Duke is one of the most difficult roles I do," he says, "but the music helps me a lot. He loves Gilda because she's a virgin, the Countess Ceprano because she's another man's wife, and Maddalena because she's a prostitute. The Duke's a dirty Don Giovanni."

Although he favors no particular role, he tends to be partial to Edgardo in *Lucia,* Arturo in *Puritani,* Nemorino in *L'Elisir d'Amore,* and, of course, Rodolfo in *La Bohème.* That is, for the present. All these parts, and the others he has been singing, fall into the lyric tenor repertory. Currently, he is engaged in both extending and expanding his repertory to include some of the heavier roles. As usual, he is going about this process very deliberately. His first journey into foreign territory was as Rodolfo in *Luisa Miller* in San Francisco in 1974. In 1975 he will tackle Manrico in *Il Trovatore* (again in San Francisco), a much heavier assignment, and if it works he will, in essence, be beginning a new phase in his professional life. "I'll be in the middle of my career because twenty-five more operas will be waiting," he says.

Pavarotti will also, no doubt, come into sharp criticism for striving to enlarge his repertory when he is so splendidly suited to the work he is doing. But it is understandable that the tenor wants to conquer new, and perhaps more exciting, fields, and no one really knows what effect—except one— the gutsier music will have on his voice. That is, Pavarotti is fully cognizant that by singing more dramatic material, he will probably be unable to return to operas like *Puritani* with their very special upper-register demands.

"The D-flat you must forget when you begin *Trovatore* and *Tosca*," he explains. "The D-flat is possible in the Bellini repertory which is legato and *leggiero*. Verdi is *espressivo*. You have to give more power. Because of this you lose one or two notes at the top." Will Pavarotti miss these strato-spheric excursions? "It's difficult to say," the tenor answers honestly. "Lauri-Volpi sang until seventy, I think, with the top very easy singing D-flats. But generally the singer whose voice is that way in old age is not really a bel canto singer. Lauri-Volpi had a superb, beautiful voice. I don't think it would offend him to say it was not really bel canto. For me, the real bel canto singers were Gigli, di Stefano, Schipa, and Pertile."

But his all-time favorite tenor, the one whom he respects the most, is, not surprisingly, Enrico Caruso. "It took me twenty years to listen better to his records," Pavarotti admits. "The first times I wasn't impressed because I was expecting good, stereophonic sound. But now I know what he is. The phrasing, the involvement, is always close to the truth—sincere with a great voice. Everytime I hear this man, I always discover something. After Caruso, my preferred tenor is my good friend Giuseppe di Stefano. I know him very well, and talk to him for many hours about singing. His phrasing must be copied because it's absolutely perfect.

And the finesse of him as a musician is, for me, incredible because it is natural, the total line, the little phrase. You know who teach him this? Nobody.

"Between Caruso and di Stefano there are Gigli, Pertile, Schipa, and Bjoerling—all, in their way, great." Does Pavarotti, as an Italian, find Bjoerling, the Swede, cold? "I find him not hot. There's a difference. I heard the tape of his last Carnegie Hall concert, two years before he died. I said to myself, anybody can die in two years. He was so strong and full of voice, it was coming from everywhere. He was not a man to die in such a short time."

Pavarotti himself has been described by critics and voice buffs as being everything from the next Caruso to this generation's Bjoerling. There is no doubt that he continues the line of great, traditional Italianate singing, but to compare him to any of the legendary singers is futile. Like all great art, his is original, although facets of it may be reminiscent of a past glory. Surely his Calaf on the *Turandot* recording is as close, at least on records, as anyone has come to Bjoerling, but in another part, Rodolfo in *La Bohème*, for example, he is much less similar.

He is unique in that, for so youthful a tenor, he is embarking on a full-fledged recitalist's career. Italians in general tend to avoid a serious preoccupation with the Mediterranean equivalent of a lieder evening. Of course, there are some notable exceptions to this rule—Schipa, Gigli, Tagliavini, di Stefano—but few began as young or with the remarkable success of Pavarotti.

Interestingly, he had a very early, unexpected, and indelible introduction to the art of song. It came following an operatic performance when he was eleven years old. "I went to see *Lucia* with Paliughi and Gigli because a baritone from my city was singing. He was a great actor, and I was more impressed with him than with the other two. I remember saying to myself, what is this great Gigli? He's not so great. But after the opera was finished, they brought a piano on stage and he sang twenty-five pieces, and then I understood very well why he was great.

"The sound of the voice was honey from top to bottom. It was romantic, very sweet, beautiful, inimitable. It was not that big—a lyric voice with the open sound of a dramatic tenor. Everybody who tries to imitate him falls down. After that concert, he immediately became a hero for me. During the *Lucia,* he came out, stayed on one side, and sang without moving even one hand. He sang great, *fabalos,* but not like the concert. This he did in the way of the greatest singers, so incredibly involved. I think he saved himself for the concert. He was fifty-seven or fifty-eight—no joke. But the voice was very fresh."

Pavarotti realizes that most singers start concertizing at the end of their careers, but is not quite sure it makes sense. "Generally they do this because opera is too heavy," he says. "But I have to tell you, I don't know what is heavier. To sing twenty or twenty-five pieces is much more difficult than one opera. I talk about artistically, vocally, and physically. You know, there's quite a lot of movement in a recital, going and coming, coming and going."

The tenor's major reason for hitting the recital trail at this point in his career is, as he has said, "to go to the people who cannot come to me." This should in no way be interpreted as a charitable gesture. Just as everything about Pavarotti must be multiplied by at least two, so is his yearning for wide public adoration limitless. Of course, it's hard to believe that even he, in his wildest imaginings, ever dreamed of the kind of response his solo appearances would generate.

His very first recital took place on February 1, 1973, in Liberty, Missouri. Pavarotti wasn't feeling well, but he sang anyway. "It was a fantastic experience," he recalls. "I arrived in Kansas City and saw the bank Jesse James took the money from. Then I stayed in the Presidential Suite, which had a piano Truman played on. Sixteen presidents slept there. I have to tell you that the presidents of America must be very strong people because the bed was so hard—God!—it was almost impossible to sleep."

As for the concert itself, "the college students didn't know me, but it was beautiful. I was no more nervous than usual, except for being sick. I know one thing: If I'm well, I can sing three days in a row. If I'm not well, I'm nervous, but I can still sing at a good level." After Liberty, he flew to Dallas and repeated the program, then had a ten-day rest before Carnegie Hall and his New York debut as a recitalist.

The concert was completely sold out. In fact, within a few days after the first newspaper announcement of the event, an unheard of $7,000, in checks and money orders was received by Pavarotti's manager. By the night of February 18, it was the hottest ticket in town.

It was also pretty hot at the Hotel Navarro, where the cause of all this excitement keeps a penthouse suite whenever he is in New York. "Suddenly I realized how important this is for me," Pavarotti says, reliving the afternoon before the night of the concert. "I was beginning to look at my watch at three, hoping it was eight. Every five minutes I was trying my voice to see if it was still there. And playing the piano. My wife was there, very nice like all the ladies, and asking the most stupid things in the world. When they are normal, the ladies are very sweet, but the moment they try to help you, they ask the most incredible things. I

Luciano Pavarotti with his wife Adua and their three daughters (*left to right*) Cristina, Giuliana, and Lorenza (*Photo by Erika Davidson*)

laughed at her questions and said, thank you for trying to help. No one can help!"

That none of the headlines the next day read "Helen Morgan Returns in Guise of Overweight Tenor" is a tribute to the sobriety of the New York music critics. Even to one who had never seen him before, it was obvious that Pavarotti initially had the jitters. To calm his nerves, and to give him something to hold onto, the tenor kept a white handkerchief in one or both his hands throughout the entire ordeal. Actually, he must have gone through a number of them, such was the twisting and mopping of sweaty brow and face that went on.

The tenor explains that he needed the mini security blanket because "at a concert you must stay more still than is possible. The best way of not moving is to keep your hands together. But you can't do this if you're holding a handkerchief. It's more natural this way, I think, and more practical. If I sweat, I can use it too. I put a lot of Pierre Cardin cologne on it and it smells beautiful."

Pavarotti could have come out in a straitjacket and the audience wouldn't have cared. Within no time, the fever pitch built, and the screamers were proving that it's not only rock fans who can whip up a vocal storm. Pavarotti has sung better and, no doubt, will sing better than he did that night, but it made no difference. That the program consisted mostly of songs and only a few operatic selections didn't get in the way, either. The all-encompassing hysteria that reared its head at Carnegie Hall was just further proof that the Big P. owns the brand of charisma and spawns the kind of ferment that made Judy Garland concerts the unique Events they were.

It's a phenomenon worth studying. Four months later, again at Carnegie Hall, Pavarotti appeared as a soloist with

the Festival Casals of Puerto Rico, singing five arias accompanied by an orchestra under the direction of Victor
Tevah. The program also consisted of symphonic pieces
interspersed between the tenor's selections. Most of the
audience, of course, was there because of Pavarotti, and
it would be reasonable to guess that the majority of them
had been to very few orchestral concerts. Such are the
vagaries of voice freaks. But they sat very patiently and
appreciatively through Haydn's Symphony No. 92 before
they got to hear their darling.

Then, once he appeared, the entire personality of the
concert changed. Electricity was in the air. And it is not
unkind to say that conductor Tevah benefited from it
mightily. His performance of Borodin's Second Symphony
—no great audience-rouser—was greeted with the kind of
cheers he has probably never received before, surely not
for this work. And at the close of the evening, the maestro
too got his share of bravos, which had less to do with his
accompaniments, which were perfectly acceptable, and
more to do with his being caught up in the storm of love
which rocked the stage that night.

Even Pavarotti is taken aback by the ferocious response
to his solo appearances. "I never saw anything like that all
for me," he says honestly. "I've seen a public like that in a
beautiful performance, but it is for all the performers, not
just for one. They touched me very much, *molto*. An
audience screaming like animals is the best payment for
the sacrifices a singer makes. At that moment, you know
you have done something for other people. To make people
behave like that, you have to do something. I'm not saying
ha, ha, ha, the public adores me. Yes, I suppose I mean it
this way too, but the real way is to be sure you have done
something for other people. Music by itself is very good,

but by itself it's not so important. It becomes important when it's doing something, going to somebody. When people scream like that, I can be sure I have done what's in my mind."

Pavarotti has no psychological problems adjusting to or accepting this kind of often overpowering mass approval. On the contrary, he revels in it. And in his own rather touching and simple way, he is very grateful for it. "Singers who cannot enjoy success are people who cannot enjoy life," he philosophizes. "There cannot exist a job better than ours. Working in art in general is the maximum thing. It's a profession because it gives you money, and it's an art because it gives you satisfaction. In the case of singers, the public—worldwide—gives us answers immediately to what we are doing. Painters sometimes have to wait a lifetime.

"Of course, singers are not real artists in terms of creation. The art is Verdi. Maria Callas is the interpreter, the second product of the art. It's artistic for sure, but for me pure art is creation. But perhaps we singers are even more lucky. We don't have the troubles composers have."

But singers do have their problems, and tenors in particular are traditionally the ones most beset by difficulties. Down through the years, operatic lore has invented and fostered a mythical, rather negative but comical, state of mind known as "the tenor mentality." This refers to everything about high-voiced males, from their being exceedingly twitchy and inordinately vain to their not having much brain matter. Legend has it that the greater the tenor, the stupider he is because when one sings in the upper reaches, the sound resonates in the cavities of the head. And tenors are supposed to have endless space up there. Another age-old legend is that tenors have to be extremely mindful of their sexual activity, that prowess in the bedroom often leads to disaster in the theater, particularly when it comes to reaching for top notes.

Pavarotti is much too bright ever to be accused of possessing a typical tenor's mentality. He is also much too fond of having a good time to cramp his style by forever worrying about *la voce*. As opposed to a run-of-the-mill tenor, for example, he thrives on fresh air and always has the windows wide open, leaving himself prone to drafts, which are the most dreaded things in a tenor's existence. The first words out of his mouth as he steps into a limousine on his way to the Met one night are, "Air-conditioning immediately please." This giant is no chicken-livered fraidy cat.

The sexual issue is something else. Pavarotti, it seems, would be delightfully content to have the reputation of being a tireless lady's man. He is always seemingly on the make and flirts with the natural abandon of a Latin lover. He is also a great kisser, and is not willing to settle for a peck on the cheek. But how much of this Valentino façade is playacting or the real thing is hard to determine. A close friend, who sees him frequently after hours, guesses that, "Luciano doesn't have an active sex life. His weight alone would make it difficult."

The tenor himself once announced during a general discussion of sex and its effect on a performer that, "I have to be very careful. It's better not to do on the day of a performance and even the day before." But on another occasion, perhaps more relaxed, he contradicted himself. "If my wife arrives after six months, I can make love the same day of a performance of *Daughter of the Regiment* and still sing beautifully. It's a physical thing. Use is not bad; abuse is bad. To use is made from God, and is something very, very perfect. We are young—it's ridiculous to feel otherwise. If you do, you are lost. Then you can't make love the day before because you are careful, and you don't make love the day after because you are tired."

Within the exaggerated framework of his own overblown personality, Pavarotti is quite sane and reasonable. One must sometimes overlook the smiling, jesting, and childlike exterior to see beyond to a man whose insights reveal a sensitivity, vulnerability, and scope, if not necessarily great depth. "You know," he muses, "when a tenor is singing very high notes, in that moment he's a little child. For him it is necessary to have protection. Even if it's not for real, because when he goes out, he's alone. But he needs to have the sensation of being protected. This is the reason that in very difficult operas, I always prefer a known conductor to a very young one. Even if the older man is not as good, his experience is better. A young conductor generally thinks everything in the world is possible, but experience teaches the older one something else."

Pavarotti makes no bones about his conductorial preferences. He would settle for Herbert von Karajan every time. "For Italian singers, it is very difficult to sing *piano*," he says. "You know why? Because in our mind the *piano* don't exist because conductors can't make a real *piano* with the orchestra. So the singers are always afraid they won't be heard. I remember very well a *Bohème* rehearsal of Karajan's. The girl singing Mimì was very loud. He said to her, please try this phrase *piano*. She said okay, but sang it *forte* again. Finally Karajan said to her, if you sing *piano*, I'll have the orchestra play *piano* and everybody will hear you. If you sing *forte*, I will have the orchestra play *forte* and you'll never be heard in the first row.

"That's just one of the things Karajan teaches you. You can be confident with a *piano* because you know somebody is there who understands what you are doing. Also, he is always with your breathing, and pauses are one of the most important things in music. He's *fabalos*, because he inspires you. There are four or five others like him. The others are afraid they won't be heard or will be accused of being accompanists."

Pavarotti believes that singers today are a far cry from their predecessors and that this, in essence, has altered the world of opera considerably. "Thirty years ago, if you were a great artist, it was better, but if you were just a great singer, it was still enough to have a big career. A lot of great singers from the past were not good artists. Now, I don't say all the singers of the present are good artists, but they must be artists to be acceptable. The level of music has changed. Now singers are more musicians than in the past, no doubt. Of course, now the voice is less important than in the past.

"Taste is different today. The public now is looking at TV ten hours a day. They see the greatest movies, the greatest acting, and they compare it to the opera stage. Today, you must be something on the stage, not just a singer because if you are just a singer, you are lost. You must communicate in a way, artistically speaking, to convince the public. If the public is not with you, *niente da fare*. It's something I feel and cannot stay without. If one night I communicate less, I know it and feel very bad. But the responsibility is on me, not the public."

No hero, Pavarotti does not always feel that total responsibility for an operatic performance must rest squarely on his broad shoulders. And when he gets down to the nitty-gritty of performance conditions around the world today, he unearths an attitude of negativism that is a side of his character usually kept under wraps. Uncomfortable in this guise, he speaks forthrightly, but with some difficulty.

"Unfortunately, I think the story of the theater is going to be finished very soon. I don't know why; it's an instinctive feeling I can't explain. And I'm speaking in general, not about the Metropolitan or La Scala. But, for example, some theaters don't do new productions of operas just because they have no money or no time or union problems. The union problems must be; everybody needs to have more money to live. But how can a man take the responsibility of saying he is doing his best if he can't say that tomorrow the orchestra will play one hour more. He can't! You know, a great conductor like Carlo Maria Giulini don't do opera anymore. You know why? Not because he don't like it. But because it's not possible to work in this way. Why is it difficult to have Karajan around the world now? Because he wants to do exactly as he wants. A production is made from a great conductor, first of all, then from a great stage director and great singers. If all these things are not going together at the same time, if you have a great conductor and stage director and all second-class singers, then you will have a second-class production.

"I think I am an important singer at the Metropolitan. But for my first *Elisir*, they didn't take care to give me any rehearsals on the stage, because they had already done this earlier. This is stupid! If the performance is sold out, there must be a reason. And we must at this point give the very best to the public in return for what they give us. There is a wonderful public all around the world, beautiful, young, and enthusiastic, who wants to drink music, real music. We are not to disappoint all these people. Remember always, to make music for everybody must be a sacrifice, not just a joy. If you have to stay three hours more to rehearse, you must. And you don't have to be paid more. I don't say the others, the orchestra and the chorus, must do the same.

Luciano Pavarotti at a radio interview (*Photo by Erika Davidson*)

I understand such a schedule will kill them, but a little flexibility is most sympathetic, and of this they must be proud, not afraid."

The idealistic Pavarotti even surprises himself. "Look," he says, a normal beam returning to his face, "generally when my feeling is pessimistic, it's not going as bad as I think." Whatever, it is curious to see an ivory-tower side to a man whose feet are usually planted firmly within the technicolored reality he has created for himself. And it is a reality. For example, despite his delight in indulging himself in daily Lucullan repasts and of being the last of the red hot operatic fatsos, he is fully cognizant of the fact that the 300-plus poundage he carries is doing him nothing but harm. "After I sing *Trovatore* for two or three years, I will stop to sing for six months," he announces aggressively. "I will lose from 50 to 100 pounds, and I don't care what happens to the voice." And where does he envision shedding all this weight? "In a prison for sure. I must."

It's hard to envision Luciano Pavarotti either imprisoned or thin.

# Index

197